SMOKING MEAT MADE EASY

SMOKING MEAT
MADE EASY

RECIPES AND TECHNIQUES TO MASTER BARBECUE

AMANDA MASON

Photography by Darren Muir

ROCKRIDGE
PRESS

For general information on our other products and services or to obtain technical support, please contact our Customer Care Department within the United States at (866) 744-2665, or outside the United States at (510) 253-0500.

Rockridge Press publishes its books in a variety of electronic and print formats. Some content that appears in print may not be available in electronic books, and vice versa.

Interior and Cover Designer: Diana Haas
Art Producer: Meg Baggott
Editor: Gurvinder Singh Gandu
Photography © 2020 Darren Muir.
Author photo courtesy of Brad Reed Photography

ISBN: Print 978-1-64739-860-6 | eBook 978-1-64739-861-3
R0

To my husband, Greg, who supports and loves me in all I do; my children, Kyliegh and Davis, you both are my greatest accomplishments; my dad, my smoking buddy, I'm thankful for all the time and memories; and my mom, who taught me I can do anything.

CONTENTS

INTRODUCTION viii

CHAPTER 1: **WHERE THERE'S SMOKE, THERE'S FLAVOR** 1

CHAPTER 2: **PORK** 36

CHAPTER 3: **BEEF & LAMB** 64

CHAPTER 4: **POULTRY** 90

CHAPTER 5: **FISH & SEAFOOD** 116

CHAPTER 6: **SIDES, SAUCES, RUBS & MARINADES** 136

MEASUREMENT CONVERSIONS 161

REFERENCES 162

INDEX 166

INTRODUCTION

ONE OF MY EARLIEST MEMORIES of my dad featured the big hole in the ground that he, my grandfather, and my uncles dug to smoke a whole hog. I couldn't have been more than five or six years old, but I remember my grandfather telling them, "Put your hand over the wood and coals, where the meat is lying on the crate. You should be able to comfortably hold your hand there without it getting too hot. That's how you know the temperature is just right for smoking."

Back then, that's how they used to measure and manage the temperature when smoking meat. They didn't have the fancy digital meat thermometers we have today. They had to control the temperature by moving the coals around, creating and minimizing airflow, and using homegrown methods like holding your hand over the fire. If I'm being honest, that all seems pretty complicated.

Smoking has come such a long way since then. I was born and raised in Tennessee, and, as you may have gleaned from the story about my grandfather, I've been around smoked food since I was a little girl. From digging holes in the ground to using a charcoal smoker, I've experienced it all. (Yes, we even have smokehouses that still get used back home.) I now live on the West Coast, and although I miss the days of hanging around outside with family and friends smoking meat all day long, I appreciate the ease of both my gas smoker and my Traeger grill.

In today's world, it's actually *easy* to smoke meat! And it doesn't have to be intimidating and overwhelming anymore. It should be fun and rewarding—and delicious! Smoking meat at home has never been more approachable, regardless of your cooking experience or the type of smoker you're using.

I've written this book as an easy-to-follow resource to help you navigate the ins and outs of smoking meat and the different techniques that can be used. I'm a big believer in smoking meat low and slow. That means you will be smoking at a low temperature over a longer time. If you want incredibly flavorful and tender meat, low and slow is the way to go! That's the secret to success. But don't worry—I'm not going to have you smoking meat for 16 to

24 hours a day. All the recipes featured in this book are considered easy and average about four hours of smoking time.

I'll focus on teaching you everything you need to know about getting started without the intimidation and hassle, and there's nothing complicated about making my recipes. If you're a beginner who has always wanted to learn how to smoke meat, you're in the right place. If you're somewhat experienced and want to dive a little bit deeper into the different types of smokers, types of woods, and why all that matters, then this book is for you as well!

Before you turn to the recipes in this book, I *highly* recommend that you start by reading chapter 1. It's an easy read that covers the basics of smoking meat and introduces tips and tricks for success. You're going to quickly see how easy and delicious it is to smoke meat! I'm so glad you're here, and I can't wait to go on this journey with you.

WHERE THERE'S SMOKE, THERE'S FLAVOR

Let's start by discussing some of the basics around smoking meat and what that means. The concept of smoking meat has been around since the Stone Age, when it was used as a technique to preserve food from spoiling. Some restaurants still smoke meat as a way to preserve food, but that's not the primary reason people smoke meat in today's world. Everyday people like you and me smoke food because we want that distinct smoky flavor and super tender, juicy meat.

Smoking is the process of cooking food in an enclosed environment by exposing it to indirect heat over wood, coal, or charcoal briquettes, which are heated before the food is added. So, what's so special about smoking meat? I'm glad you asked! When using a smoker to cook meat, the air temperature is raised and can be controlled. Smoking at a lower heat than your typical grill or oven raises the temperature of the meat slowly until it is fully cooked. The smoke produced during this process sets this cooking method apart from others. While smoking meat adds a ton of flavor, it also keeps the meat juicy and tender by trapping in moisture during the cooking process.

When people hear the phrase "smoking meat," the first thing they likely think about is how many hours they're going to have to sit around, managing the temperature of the smoker. While that approach is necessary depending on the type of smoker you use, the cut of meat being smoked, and how much meat you're smoking, it's not my typical approach.

Don't get me wrong—there are times when you will find me out on the back porch with my dad smoking a 20-pound pork shoulder that takes around 24 hours to complete, but I don't do that every day. I like to light my smoker, throw on a couple of steaks or pieces of chicken, and be ready to eat around two to three hours later. And that's my main approach in this book: We're going to focus on the basics so you can get *amazing* results every single time you use your smoker.

RULES FOR MEAT SMOKING SUCCESS

I've spent a lot of time around the smoker, and I've smoked all kinds of different foods. As I mentioned earlier, my dad introduced me to the concept of smoking meat when I was young and, ever since then, I've spent many hours thinking about and discussing smoking methods, different types and cuts of meats to smoke, and rubs to add flavor.

In practicing the art of smoking over many years, I've developed a philosophy about the practice. These are my keys to success:

THE MEAT IS THE STAR OF THE SHOW. Identifying the type of meat you want to smoke and understanding what comes along with it is super important right from the start. For example, smoking a whole chicken is going to take a lot less time and effort than smoking a 22-pound brisket. Knowing the basics for different types of meat will set you up for success.

LOW AND SLOW. Smoking the meat at a low temperature for a certain length of time gives you a flavor and texture that can only be achieved with this method of cooking. Smoking on low heat allows the fat to render into the meat, giving it a flavor and texture that stands out. The higher the temperature, the higher the risk of the meat drying out.

CONTROLLING THE HEAT. To get the desired results from smoking, you have to control the heat in the smoker. A steady smoking temperature is important for obtaining tender, flavorful meats. For most low and slow cooking, you need to know how to get your smoker's temperature between 225°F and 250°F and keep it in that range for the duration of the smoke time.

SMOKE AND WOOD. When heated, the wood produces smoke, which cooks the meat and gives it the trademark barbecue smell and flavor. Using flavored wood provides a lot of flavor when smoking meat. Learning how to generate a good smoke will take your smoking game to the next level.

RUBS AND SAUCES. A rub is a mixture of ingredients that are mixed and applied to the outside of meat. Rubs can either be wet or dry and typically has either a sweet or salty base. While rubs are not required when smoking meat, they produce a lot of flavor and have a direct effect on creating the outer bark, or crust, on the meat.

EQUIPMENT. Besides the smoker itself, there's no other "required" equipment for smoking. Having the right tools, however, does make the smoking process so much easier. Investing in these tools will also improve the quality of the food you're smoking. (More on this shortly.)

PRACTICE, PRACTICE, PRACTICE! Smoking is both an art and a science. When first starting out, it's all about trial and error. It's normal to make mistakes because that's how you'll learn and start to develop your own techniques. If this is your first time smoking, I would recommend starting with a whole chicken. It's an inexpensive piece of meat, cooks evenly, and has a shorter smoke time.

TYPES OF SMOKERS

All the recipes I've created in this cookbook can be made using any type of smoker; even a standard grill can be used as a makeshift smoker if you're not quite sure you want to invest in smoking equipment yet. For these recipes, you only need one smoker—and any kind will do. I have a few types of smokers that serve different purposes. For example, there are times when I want smoked meat, but I don't necessarily have the patience or time to babysit the temperature control component on my charcoal or gas smoker. That's when

I use my pellet smoker. And let me tell you, it's so easy to smoke on a pellet smoker. I like to use that during the week for easy smokes and my gas or charcoal smoker on the weekends when I have more time to manage the process. When I want to actually take the time to experience the type of smoking I did when I was growing up, I use my gas smoker. It requires a little bit more work to prepare the water pan and wood chunks and monitor the temperature, but it's a process I enjoy.

There are a lot of different smokers on the market, so it can often be difficult to determine which one is best for you. In this book, I'm only presenting the ones I consider easy to use.

CHARCOAL SMOKERS. While charcoal smokers are still popular today, they are more difficult to manage than other smokers. An open fire is used and the heat is managed by controlling multiple air vents and moving charcoal briquettes around. I find it difficult to maintain the temperature with a charcoal smoker over a long period of time, but many people prefer this method. While it requires a lot of monitoring, one of the benefits to using a charcoal smoker is how amazing the meat tastes once it's done. The meat tends to come out a bit more charred, and the flavor is just phenomenal. The price range for charcoal smokers shows that they're much more affordable, typically between $50 and $400.

PROPANE GAS SMOKERS. One of the benefits of this type of smoker is that you don't have to worry about the temperature of the charcoal briquettes and ensuring that it's hot enough before you put the meat in the smoker. This smoker runs off a propane gas tank. My gas smoker is vertical and comes with five removable racks and small hooks for conveniently hanging sausages. Having a vertical gas smoker makes my smoking experience a lot easier because I can smoke different types of meat all at once. I tend to get a good smoke with this type of smoker, which intensifies the flavor of the food even more. You'll typically see vertical gas smokers but there are some that are horizontal in shape. These smokers tend to be very cost-effective, ranging anywhere from $150 to $550.

ELECTRIC SMOKERS. While I love the monitoring and maintenance involved with both charcoal and propane gas smokers, an electric smoker is a good option for those who are just starting out on their smoking journey. They come with a digital control panel that lets you start the smoker and set the time and temperature. Electric smokers come with a water pan and a wood chip container. I only recommend using wood chips with an electric smoker. There's typically just not enough heat to get chunks of wood smoking and if there are too many wood chunks, you could start a fire. One of the features I love the most when using an electric smoker is that some models come with a digital remote control, which makes smoking extremely convenient. From a cost perspective, electric smokers can range anywhere from $300 to $9,000.

PELLET SMOKERS. If you're looking for an easy, convenient, low-maintenance smoking experience, consider going with a pellet smoker. It offers the flavor of a wood-based smoker with the convenience of a gas grill. One of the biggest perks to using this type of smoker is that it provides regulated temperature control. Pellet smokers are electric and must be plugged into an outside power outlet. If you like the concept of "set it and forget it," you'll enjoy using a pellet smoker. It's perfect for anyone who wants to conveniently smoke meat without all the hassle of controlling the temperature, wood chips, and water pan. You can also grill, bake, and roast in a pellet smoker. And I love the temperature range—it goes as low as 180°F and can be raised all the way up to 500°F. Pellet smokers tend to be a bit more expensive, ranging from $300 to $9,000.

HOW TO SMOKE MEAT USING A STANDARD GRILL

My dad has a gas smoker but often uses a standard barbecue grill to smoke meat. Turning a standard grill into a smoker is relatively easy and effective. Here's how:

1. To get started, you'll need to heat some charcoal briquettes. The easiest way to do this is by filling a chimney starter with the briquettes.

2. Fill the chimney starter until it's about a third of the way full, which should be between 25 and 30 briquettes. When the briquettes are ready, they will turn light gray. You'll also see an orange-red color in the charcoal briquettes.

3. Once the briquettes are hot, you'll be ready to assemble your standard grill for indirect smoking. To do this, put a disposable aluminum pan directly on one side of the wire rack inside the grill. This will be used as a water pan.

4. On the other side of the grill, pour the hot briquettes directly onto the metal rack. Make sure the briquettes are stacked on top of one another to help generate heat and keep the temperature hot inside the grill.

5. Next, put a handful of wood chips (about 1 cup) on top of the briquettes.

6. Put the grill grate over the water pan and briquettes.

7. Put the lid on the grill and open the vent on top of the lid about a quarter of the way to allow airflow. If the grill has a bottom vent, it should also be opened a quarter of the way.

WOOD AND OTHER FUEL SOURCES

We've all heard that wood is an important component when it comes to smoking meat, but you may have wondered what role it plays in the smoking process. Depending on what type of smoker you use, the wood and fuel sources will differ. Let's break down the different types of wood and fuel sources needed for each commonly used smoker type.

CHARCOAL SMOKERS are another way to smoke food with indirect heat generated by burning—you guessed it—charcoal. Coal isn't typically used anymore because it gets too hot. Charcoal briquettes are used instead because they burn at the proper temperature for grilling and smoking purposes. Wood chips can also be added to the charcoal briquettes to produce a smokier flavor. When using a charcoal smoker, a water pan is needed to help maintain temperature control. The heat source for a charcoal smoker is a direct flame, and the temperature is managed with air vents built into the smoker. Once the charcoal briquettes are lit, a fire will slowly burn down until the charcoal briquettes are covered in a thin white ash. The meat is then placed directly on the grill grates. The flavor a charcoal smoker produces is hands-down tastier than when using a gas, electric, or pellet smoker. You'll get more of that deep smoke and charred flavor that people desire.

ELECTRIC SMOKERS must be plugged into an outdoor power outlet so that it can cook the food via electricity. This type of smoker works by heating a cooking chamber where air circulates and heats the meat via convection. There are built-in fans that bring in the air, which then directs the heat and smoke to the cooking area. Wood chips can also be used.

GAS SMOKERS use a propane gas tank for the fuel source and wood to produce heat. Either flavored wood chips or chunks can be used. To ignite, the hose from the smoker gets securely attached to the propane tank, very similar to what you do with a gas grill. The wood is then placed in its designated pan and typically positioned directly above the flame; when ignited, the wood becomes hot and produces smoke. A water pan should also be placed above the wood tray in the gas smoker. The water pan plays an important part in a gas smoker. According to Craig Goldwyn, the *New York Times* bestselling author of *Meathead: The Science of Great Barbecue and Grilling*, a water pan will "stabilize the temperature inside the grill." This means that when the water gets hot enough, it will radiate heat up toward the meat if the temperature in the smoker begins to lower. It also works the other way around. The water will absorb excess heat if the smoker starts to get too hot. You'll get a nice output of smoky flavor to your meat when you use a gas smoker.

PELLET SMOKERS have no direct flame and get their fuel from electricity and wood pellets. Wood pellets are poured into the chamber and ignited by electricity. There are built-in fans that bring in the air, which then directs the heat and smoke to the cooking area. A pellet smoker has the ability to provide both direct and indirect heat, fueled by a combination of wood pellets and electricity. While the pellets do produce smoke, you're not going to get the same smoky flavor that a gas or charcoal smoker produces. It's similar but not as intense.

WOOD FLAVORS

When it comes to using wood for everyday food smoking purposes, you'll either use chips, chunks, or wood pellets. When I use my gas smoker, I typically use wood chunks instead of wood chips.

Chips are thin pieces of wood shavings and tend to burn out pretty quickly. When smoking meat that takes around two hours, I'll use chips because they'll fully burn in this time span. When using a charcoal smoker, chips are great to mix in with the charcoal briquettes because they help produce a smoky flavor to the meat.

Wood chunks are bigger and burn slow over a longer period of time. When smoking a larger piece of meat that takes many hours, wood chunks are the way to go. And keep in mind that just because the smoker is still producing smoke doesn't mean the wood is still burning. After four to five hours of smoking, always check the wood tray to see if more is needed.

Not only does wood contribute to the fuel source, but it also provides a tremendous amount of flavor to the meat you're smoking. Here are the most commonly used wood flavors and the types of meats they're best used for:

TYPE OF WOOD	FLAVORS	USE FOR
ALDER	Mild, sweet, musky	Fish and seafood
APPLE	Mild, sweet, fruity	Pork, chicken, turkey, lamb, duck
CHERRY	Mild, sweet, fruity	Pork, chicken, fish, seafood
HICKORY	Strong, sweet, heavy bacon flavor	Pork, beef, lamb
MESQUITE	Strong, earthy smoke flavor	Pork, beef
OAK	Medium, traditional smoke flavor	Pork, beef
PECAN	Mild, sweet, similar to hickory	Pork, beef, chicken, turkey

Here is a chart of other suitable wood types you can smoke with. These are less common and may be harder to find, but you can have fun experimenting with the different flavors.

TYPE OF WOOD	FLAVORS	USE FOR
ACACIA	Similar to mesquite wood, burns very hot	Pork, beef, chicken, duck, lamb
ALMOND	Sweet	Pork, chicken, turkey, lamb, duck, beef, fish, seafood
ASH	Distinctive flavor, burns quickly	Beef, fish

TYPE OF WOOD	FLAVORS	USE FOR
APRICOT	Mild, sweet smoke flavor	Chicken, turkey, pork, fish, seafood
BIRCH	Maple flavor	Pork, chicken, turkey
GRAPEFRUIT	Mild smoke flavor	Beef, pork, fish, seafood, duck, chicken, turkey
GRAPEVINE	Tart in flavor, produces a lot of smoke	Pork, chicken, turkey, lamb, duck, beef
LEMON	Mild smoke flavor	Beef, pork, fish, seafood, duck, chicken, turkey
LILAC	Subtle, floral flavor	Lamb, fish, seafood
MAPLE	Sweet, produces a lot of smoke	Pork, chicken, turkey, duck
ORANGE	Mild smoke flavor	Beef, pork, fish, seafood, duck, chicken, turkey
PEACH	Mild, sweet smoke flavor	Chicken, turkey, pork, fish, seafood

WOOD TO AVOID

While there are many types of wood that are great for smoking, there are also certain types of woods that are not safe to use. Conifer woods are considered softwoods and are generally not safe to use to smoke meat. These woods include trees that produce cones and needles, like pine or redwood. Cedar wood is also a conifer, but salmon is often smoked on cedar planks. This smoking method is considered safe because the wood isn't being burnt but used as a flavor mechanism with indirect heat being applied.

Never use woods such as sassafras, poisonous walnut, and mangrove, as they contain toxins. Also stay away from lumber scraps. Most of the time, there are different mixtures of wood in the scraps and you never truly know the type of wood you may be burning. While it may be convenient to use wood scraps, they can still be dangerous when smoking because of potential pesticides that may have been used on the trees.

It's always best to buy your wood chips, chunks, or pellets from a trusted merchandiser. But even then you have to be careful with the wood and apply some best practices. Make sure you store the bags of wood in a cool, dry place away from sunlight so they don't mold. Purchased wood does expire, even if the bag doesn't necessarily specify that it does. Wood can get moldy and grow fungus if it's been exposed to moisture over time.

HOW TO BUILD AND FEED YOUR FIRE

Now that we've broken down the different types of wood and fuel sources needed, let's talk about building and maintaining the fire needed for smoking meat. How you build and feed the fire for indirect smoking will depend on the type of smoker you use.

CHARCOAL SMOKER

For charcoal smokers, it's going to take a bit more effort to keep the fire going because there is more involved. Regulating the temperature is important when smoking in a charcoal smoker and since you're dealing with multiple components like charcoal briquettes, wood chips, a water pan, and fire, it requires staying on top of things to ensure that just enough air is being regulated through the vents.

When using a charcoal smoker, I do find it helpful to soak wood chips for no longer than 30 minutes before smoking. Since chips burn so fast, a little soak helps them last a bit longer.

Here's a quick method you can use to build the fire using a charcoal smoker:

1. Start off by soaking a handful of wood chips (about one cup) for 30 minutes in water.

2.   Then, take about 15 to 20 unlit charcoal briquettes and dump them on one side of the smoker.

3.   Take a handful of the soaked wood chips and put them on top of the unlit charcoal briquettes.

4.   Next, you're going to take 20 to 30 charcoal briquettes that have already been heated in a chimney starter and put them directly on top of the unlit charcoal briquettes and wood chips. I like to then add another handful of soaked wood chips and put them directly on top of the lit charcoal briquettes and move it around to combine.

5.   Put the grill grate back in place and then put a water-filled pan directly above the lit charcoal briquettes. Doing so helps regulate the temperature.

6.   Then put the lid on the smoker and put a thermometer in one of the vents so you can monitor the internal temperature.

7.   When the temperature gets to be about 250°F, remove the lid and put the food on the grate on the opposite side from the direct heat source.

8.   Then put the lid back on, making sure the vents are over whatever you are cooking.

I've found that the easiest way to control the heat in a charcoal smoker is by adjusting the airflow. To get more airflow, open the air vents wider. This will result in a hotter fire. To cool the fire, partially close the vents. Another option for keeping the fire going is to build a three-zone fire. This method entails having three separate charcoal locations set up in your smoker. The first zone will be a pile of lit, very hot charcoal. The center zone of lit charcoals should be used as a moderate zone. The third zone should have unlit charcoals for a cool zone. By moving the food around to the three different zones during the smoking process, you can effectively control the heat. If you're doing a long smoke, you'll need to add more lit charcoal every two to three hours once you notice the temperature dropping.

GAS SMOKER

When using a gas smoker, it's relatively easy to feed the fire and keep it going. You should prepare the wood and water pans before igniting the flame. For less mess and easier cleanup, I recommend lining the water pan with heavy-duty aluminum foil and then adding the water to the pan once it has been placed in the smoker. There are multiple approaches for preparing the wood. Some people soak their wood before placing it in the smoker. There are a lot of opinions out there on this topic, but based on my years of experience, it isn't always necessary to soak the wood before you smoke. The thought process behind soaking wood prior to smoking is that the moisture in the wood will slow the combustion and create a better flavored, longer smoke time than if the wood wasn't soaked. What I've found is that when I soak wood, it takes a lot longer to produce smoke, and it doesn't produce as much smoke. When I use dry wood, I get an immediate smoke that lasts a long time.

To keep the fire fed, make sure you're checking the wood every four to five hours and adding more wood directly to the pan when the wood looks completely burnt or when it has turned to ash. With long smokes, it's important to keep the fire going with fresh wood. Just because the smoker is still smoking doesn't mean the wood is still burning. There's nothing worse than fueling your fire with too much smoke from burnt-out wood—your food will taste awful.

UNDERSTANDING "THIN BLUE SMOKE"

When using a charcoal or gas smoker, you can get to the point where too much smoke is being produced. There is a phrase in the barbecue world called "thin blue smoke," and this is the type of smoke you want. According to pit master Malcom Reed, "Thin blue smoke is the byproduct of clean-burning wood at just the right temperature." He also notes that this smoke makes your food taste amazing! A charcoal smoker with thick white smoke means that the bed of charcoal briquettes isn't hot enough for the amount of wood being used. When this happens, there isn't enough oxygen and too much carbon, and it produces a thick white smoke that will make your meat taste bitter. To reduce the thick white smoke, you can add more wood. It can either be prelit wood (get it started burning first in a bucket) or dry wood chips or chunks.

Both methods will aid in removing moisture (water vapor), which is primarily what causes the heavy white smoke. Also, make sure the smoker vents are wide open. The same concept holds true when using a gas smoker. If the smoke is too thick and white, add three or four more wood chunks to the wood pan. If you can't get the smoke under control, then put out the fire and start again.

ELECTRIC SMOKER

An electric smoker is very similar to the pellet smoker and doesn't require you to feed the fire. It runs off electricity to keep the temperature regulated. Wood can be used to produce smoke and flavor the food.

PELLET SMOKER

There's a designated area in the pellet smoker (typically called an auger or a pellet hopper) where the wood pellets get added and automatically feed into the smoker. You don't have to worry about feeding the fire for pellet smokers until you start running low on pellets. One of the Traeger pellet smoker models comes with an 18-pound-capacity pellet hopper, which will keep it smoking for many hours. You'll want to make sure there are always enough pellets in the hopper so you don't run out during the smoking process. Before you start, ensure the pellet hopper is at least half full. You never want to add pellets by hand to the hot firepot because it is very dangerous and can result in burns. If the pellet smoker runs out of wood pellets and loses the fire while cooking, you should let the smoker completely cool down and then start again with the initial instructions.

SMOKING EQUIPMENT

When starting, you might think you don't need or want to invest in a smoker, and although it's true that you can use your standard grill to smoke food, having a smoker will give you the authentic experience and taste of smoked food. There are also a few tools and accessories that can enhance your smoking experience.

Just like anything else in life, having the right type of equipment can make the job so much easier. While it's true that you only need the smoker, and, depending on the type, either wood, charcoal, or both to get started, there's a lot of other tools you should consider using to elevate your experience. When it comes to smoking meat, accessories are important. Not only do they help you become better at smoking, but they also help improve the quality and taste of your meat.

ESSENTIALS

The following list are things I consistently use for smoking meat:

ALUMINUM FOIL: Essential for wrapping the water pan, wood pan, and meat. I use both regular foil and the longer rolls of heavy-duty foil.

GALLON-SIZE RESEALABLE PLASTIC BAGS: Used for brining pieces of meat before smoking. Always put the bag in a large bowl while it's brining to catch any leaks.

BARBECUE GRILL BASKET: Needed for certain recipes like pork belly burnt ends, brisket burnt ends, and duck.

DISPOSABLE ALUMINUM PANS: Used when smoking certain meats such as pork and beef burnt ends as well as for several seafood dishes.

BAKING SHEETS: Used when smoking sliced bacon and certain seafood.

WIRE RACK: Aids in proper air flow and allows fat to drip when smoking meats such as bacon and duck.

DIGITAL MEAT THERMOMETER: Gauges the internal temperature of the meat while smoking.

HEAT-RESISTANT GLOVES/OVEN MITTS: Reduces the risk of burning your hands and arms when reaching into the smoker and removing the meat.

DISPOSABLE GLOVES: When you're slathering on a rub to a raw piece of meat, gloves reduce the mess.

BARBECUE TONGS: Needed for removing meat from the smoker.

BASTING BRUSH: An easy way to apply basting liquid during the smoking process.

GRILL BRUSH: Helps with cleaning the smoker racks.

CUTTING BOARD: Used to slice smoked meat.

SPRAY BOTTLE: Spray water directly onto the wood after smoking is finished to ensure a fire doesn't start.

FIRE EXTINGUISHER: Have a fire extinguisher near your smoking area at all times so you can easily access it in case your smoker fire gets out of control.

UPGRADES

While not necessary, investing in certain add-ons and tools can upgrade your smoking skills even more. Here are a few to consider:

COLD SMOKER GENERATOR: When you get comfortable with smoking basic meats, you may find yourself wanting to cold smoke other foods such as cheese. A cold smoker generator allows food to smoke consistently at temperatures as low as 80°F to 120°F.

SEAR BOX ATTACHMENT: This tool will attach to your pellet smoker and is great for searing meat before placing it on the smoker.

SIDEKICK: A more versatile attachment for your pellet smoker, the sidekick will not only sear, but it will also grill, sauté, boil, and fry foods.

CONTROL FAN: Great for use with a charcoal smoker. It helps minimize flareups and burn-outs and reduces the need to make vent adjustments and tend to the charcoal during the smoking process.

OFFSET SMOKER: This is an upgraded smoker that typically has a longer chamber where you can smoke a lot of food at once. Offset smokers also have a firebox attached to the side so you can add more fuel without opening the cooking chamber. They are typically made of thick steel, which helps retain heat and stabilize temperatures.

CHIMNEY STARTER: This tool is used to ignite either lump charcoal or charcoal briquettes.

THE MEAT SMOKER'S PANTRY

Every at-home pitmaster (that's you!) needs a well-stocked pantry filled with ingredients for all your barbecue and smoking needs. There are certain staple ingredients I always have stocked on my shelves. I make sure I have at least two of each ingredient because there's nothing worse than having to run to the grocery store when you're in the middle of making a recipe. Whether I'm creating new rubs, new brines, or just want to have extra of my favorite dry rubs already premade, I keep these ingredients in stock and on my shelves at all times.

DRY INGREDIENTS

BROWN SUGAR: Both light and dark brown sugar are needed for making different types of rubs and barbecue sauces.

CUMIN: This spice comes in a seed form and has a warm, earthy flavor. While the seed form works, I prefer using ground cumin in dry rubs.

CHILI POWDER: This powder has a mild to moderate spicy flavor. It is a main ingredient I use in both rubs and sauces.

GARLIC POWDER: It is made from garlic cloves that have been dehydrated and ground into a powder. I use this ingredient in the majority of my dry rubs.

ONION POWDER: This powder is made from dehydrated onions that have been ground into a fine powder. This is another ingredient I use regularly in my dry rubs.

MINCED DRIED ONIONS: The dried onions add a sweet flavor without having to use a fresh onion. I mostly use this ingredient when making barbecue sauces.

SMOKED PAPRIKA: This spice is made from chiles that are smoke-dried and then crushed, whereas regular paprika is just crushed dried chiles. It is another key ingredient used in most of my dry rubs.

MUSTARD POWDER: This powder is made from both brown and white mustard seeds and mixed with saffron and turmeric for added flavor. This key ingredient is found in my dry rubs. I also use it when making barbecue sauces.

ROSEMARY: I often use rosemary, an excellent aromatic dried spice, in pork recipes. I typically use fresh rosemary sprigs in brines and wet rubs but dried rosemary in dry rubs.

SALT: There are different types of salt—kosher, sea salt, and Himalayan salt—each with a different purpose and different flavors.

PEPPER: The four types of pepper I use are black peppercorn (whole or ground), white pepper, and cayenne. I use every kind when making different brines, sauces, and dry rubs. Each pepper provides a unique flavor.

WET INGREDIENTS

APPLE CIDER VINEGAR: This vinegar is primarily used in brines to help tenderize meats as well as when making barbecue sauce.

OLIVE OIL: I often apply extra-virgin olive oil before adding a dry rub. If I have flavor-infused olive oils on hand, I prefer to use those for added flavor.

BALSAMIC VINEGAR: Standard balsamic vinegar can be found at any grocery store and works well in all my recipes. Feel free to use a flavored balsamic vinegar if you have one on hand, as it will enhance the flavor of the dish.

BUTTER: Both salted and unsalted butter can be used when making glazes. I also rub butter onto some meats to aid in forming the bark.

KETCHUP: This ingredient is used when making barbecue sauces.

FRESH LEMON AND ORANGE: These fruits are used in brines and in a lot of my seafood recipes.

YELLOW MUSTARD: This mustard is brushed directly onto pork before smoking to aid in forming the bark.

FLAVORING YOUR MEAT

Earlier in this chapter, we talked about how different types of wood provide different flavors to the meat when smoking. And although that is true, *how* and *when* you flavor your meat with spices, brines, and marinades also makes a huge impact on taste. Many meats are very flavorful on their own (think prime rib, filet mignon, and rib eye), but there are other meats, like pork, that thrive when combined with certain marinades and spices.

Various types of flavoring methods will impact the taste based on whether you're flavoring before you begin to smoke or during the smoking process. For example, completely dunking tiger shrimp in a lemon butter sauce before you smoke will result in a different flavor than if you basted it multiple times during the smoking process. Let's dive into some of the different methods and benefits of flavoring meat before, during, and after smoking.

FLAVORING RAW MEAT

There are many benefits to flavoring raw meat before smoking, and there are several methods you can apply.

BRINE typically consists of water, fruit juice, some type of vinegar, and salt. The method of brining is often applied to leaner cuts, and although it does help tenderize the meat, it also adds flavor. Brined meat will absorb extra liquid and salt, resulting in a juicier and more flavorful smoked meat. Always brine meat in the refrigerator.

CURING is another method used when making bacon from pork belly. It's mainly done to preserve food and keep it from spoiling, but it also tends to add an extra-salty flavor. While curing is necessary for certain smoked foods, it's a long process and can be tedious. You won't need to cure any meat for the recipes found in this cookbook—we're keeping things simple and easy.

RUBS, MARINADES, AND INJECTIONS are also common and popular ways to flavor food before smoking. I tend to use a lot of dry rubs as they create that "bark" on the outside of the meat that everyone loves so much. Bark is the tasty crust that forms on certain types of smoked meat (ribs, for example) when the surface is exposed to heat and oxygen.

FLAVORING MEAT DURING AND AFTER COOKING

Flavoring certain meats during the smoking process packs in a lot of flavor. When I smoke a big ham, I baste it with a pineapple, brown sugar, and honey glaze at multiple intervals (depending on the temperature) until it's done. Not only does this add flavor, but it also helps keep the ham from drying out during smoking.

People rave about the flavor of my smoked meats and often ask me how I get the meat to be so juicy and tender. It's mainly because I wrap certain meats in foil along with a wet rub or marinade about one and a half hours before the meat is done smoking. This wrapping method provides a lot of extra flavor to the meat, and I do it often with cuts of pork including loin, tenderloin, and shoulder.

Depending on the cut, I also add sauces and glazes after the meat has finished smoking. For example, the softened butter, fresh garlic, and rosemary that was smoked with the pork loin wrapped in foil during the last one and a half hours of smoking makes an amazing gravy to pour over the pork after it's sliced. Just remember that glazes, sauces, bastes, and gravies add a ton of flavor before, during, and after smoking, and they also add a lot of extra moisture, which helps make the final product juicy and ridiculously tender.

MEAT SMOKING TIME AND TEMPERATURE

There are so many different types and cuts of meat that you can smoke, and when you're first starting out you may want to experiment with a variety of meats. You'll probably ask yourself, "Wait, what temperature do I need to smoke on for this cut of meat? And what kind of wood should I be using?" Let's be honest, it can seem a bit overwhelming.

Here's a simple chart that breaks down the essential elements you need to know when it comes to smoking meat. This chart can be used as a quick reference anytime you fire up the smoker. Please keep in mind that the numbers in the chart should serve as a general baseline, as they can vary depending on quantity of meat. More specific cooking times and temperatures are listed in each recipe.

PORK					
PROTEIN TYPE/CUT OF MEAT	ESTIMATED COOKING TIME	COOKING TEMPERATURE	DONE TEMPERATURE	REST TIME	PREFERRED WOOD
Pork Tenderloin	2 to 3 hours	225°F	145°F	3 minutes	Apple or cherry
Pork Loin	3 to 4 hours	225°F	145°F	3 minutes	Apple or cherry
Pork Shoulder/ Boston Butt, pulled	1 to 1½ hours per lb	225°F	203°F	1 hour	Apple or cherry
Hot Links/ Sausages	1 hour	225°F	165°F	3 minutes	Apple
Ham, Precooked (7 to 8lbs)	3 to 4 hours	225°F	145°F	5 minutes	Apple or cherry
Pork Belly Burnt Ends	4 to 5 hours	250°F	205°F	7 to 10 minutes	Apple or cherry
Chorizo Links	1 hour	225°F	165°F	3 minutes	Apple
Bratwurst	2 hours	225°F	160°F	3 minutes	Apple
Pit Ham	3 to 4 hours	250°F	145°F	5 minutes	Apple or cherry
Pork Spare Ribs	4 to 5 hours	225°F	203°F	10 minutes	Apple, cherry, or pecan
Ham Hock	2 hours	200°F	150°F	10 minutes	Hickory or apple
Baby Back Ribs	5 to 6 hours	225°F	190 to 203°F	10 minutes	Apple, cherry, or pecan
Pork Chops	45 minutes to 1 hour	250°F	145°F	3 minutes	Apple

BEEF					
PROTEIN TYPE/CUT OF MEAT	ESTIMATED COOKING TIME	COOKING TEMPERATURE	DONE TEMPERATURE	REST TIME	PREFERRED WOOD
Prime Rib	4 to 5 hours	225°F	Extra-rare or blue: 80 to 100°F Rare: 120 to 125°F Medium-rare: 130 to 135°F Medium: 140 to 145°F Medium-well: 150 to 155°F Well-done: 160°F and above	3 minutes	Apple, cherry, oak
Brisket	45 minutes to 1 hour per lb	225°F	180°F	1 to 2 hours	Apple, hickory
Brisket Burnt Ends	4 to 5 hours	250°F	170°F	10 minutes	Hickory, apple, cherry
Meatloaf	3 to 4 hours	225°F	165°F	5 minutes	Apple, cherry
Beef Short Ribs	5 to 6 hours	225°F	205°F	5 minutes	Hickory, apple, cherry
Top Round— Beef Jerky	3 to 4 hours	180°F	175°F	1 hour	Hickory

BEEF					
PROTEIN TYPE/CUT OF MEAT	ESTIMATED COOKING TIME	COOKING TEMPERATURE	DONE TEMPERATURE	REST TIME	PREFERRED WOOD
Tri-Tip	3 to 4 hours	250°F	Extra-rare or blue: 80 to 100°F Rare: 120 to 125°F Medium-rare: 130 to 135°F Medium: 140 to 145°F Medium-well: 150 to 155°F Well-done: 160°F and above	3 minutes	Oak, mesquite, pecan
Sirloin Tip Roast	2 to 3 hours	250°F	Extra-rare or blue: 80 to 100°F Rare: 120 to 125°F Medium-rare: 130 to 135°F Medium: 140 to 145°F Medium-well: 150 to 155°F Well-done: 160°F and above	3 minutes	Oak, hickory, mesquite

BEEF					
PROTEIN TYPE/CUT OF MEAT	ESTIMATED COOKING TIME	COOKING TEMPERATURE	DONE TEMPERATURE	REST TIME	PREFERRED WOOD
Chuck Roast	6 to 8 hours	225°F	200°F	10 minutes	Hickory, pecan
Rib Eye	2 to 3 hours	225°F	Extra-rare or blue: 80 to 100°F Rare: 120 to 125°F Medium-rare: 130 to 135°F Medium: 140 to 145°F Medium-well: 150 to 155°F Well-done: 160°F and above	3 minutes	Oak, hickory, mesquite
Filet Mignon	1 to 2 hours	225°F	Extra-rare or blue: 80 to 100°F Rare: 120 to 125°F Medium-rare: 130 to 135°F Medium: 140 to 145°F Medium-well: 150 to 155°F Well-done: 160°F and above	3 minutes	Apple, cherry, oak

BEEF					
PROTEIN TYPE/CUT OF MEAT	ESTIMATED COOKING TIME	COOKING TEMPERATURE	DONE TEMPERATURE	REST TIME	PREFERRED WOOD
Flank Steak	2 to 3 hours	225°F	Rare: 120 to 125°F Medium-rare: 130 to 135°F Medium: 140 to 145°F Medium-well: 150 to 155°F Well-done: 160°F and above	3 minutes	Oak or mesquite

LAMB					
PROTEIN TYPE/CUT OF MEAT	ESTIMATED COOKING TIME	COOKING TEMPERATURE	DONE TEMPERATURE	REST TIME	PREFERRED WOOD
Lamb Shoulder	5 to 6 hours	225°F	Medium-rare: 130 to 140°F Medium: 140 to 150°F	10 minutes	Oak, maple, apple, cherry
Lamb Loin Chops	1 to 2 hours	225°F	Medium-rare: 130 to 140°F Medium: 140 to 150°F	3 minutes	Oak, maple, apple, cherry

LAMB					
PROTEIN TYPE/CUT OF MEAT	ESTIMATED COOKING TIME	COOKING TEMPERATURE	DONE TEMPERATURE	REST TIME	PREFERRED WOOD
Lamb Burger	45 minutes to 1 hour	250°F	165°F	3 minutes	Oak, maple, apple, cherry
Rack of Lamb	1 to 2 hours	225°F	Medium-rare: 130 to 140°F Medium: 140 to 150°F	5 minutes	Oak, maple, apple, cherry

POULTRY					
PROTEIN TYPE/CUT OF MEAT	ESTIMATED COOKING TIME	COOKING TEMPERATURE	DONE TEMPERATURE	REST TIME	PREFERRED WOOD
Chicken, whole (4 to 5 lbs)	4 to 5 hours	225 to 250°F	165°F	3 to 5 minutes	Apple, cherry, maple
Chicken breasts (boneless, skinless)	2 to 3 hours	225 to 250°F	165°F	3 minutes	Apple, cherry, maple
Chicken thighs	2 to 3 hours	225 to 250°F	165°F	3 minutes	Apple, cherry, maple
Quarters (12 to 16 oz)	3 to 4 hours	225 to 250°F	165°F	3 minutes	Apple, cherry, maple
Wings (1½ to 2 lbs)	1 to 2 hours	225 to 250°F	165°F	3 minutes	Apple, cherry, maple

POULTRY					
PROTEIN TYPE/CUT OF MEAT	ESTIMATED COOKING TIME	COOKING TEMPERATURE	DONE TEMPERATURE	REST TIME	PREFERRED WOOD
Drumsticks	2 to 3 hours	225 to 250°F	165°F	3 minutes	Apple, cherry, maple
Cornish Hen	1 to 2 hours	225 to 250°F	165°F	3 minutes	Apple, cherry, maple, pecan
Turkey, whole (12 to 15 lbs)	6 to 7 hours	225 to 250°F	165°F	10 minutes	Apple, cherry, maple
Turkey Breast	3 to 4 hours	225 to 250°F	165°F	10 minutes	Apple, cherry, maple
Duck	2 to 3 hours	300°F	165°F	5 minutes	cherry, apple, oak
Quail	45 minutes to 1 hour	225°F	155°F	3 minutes	Apple, cherry

SEAFOOD					
PROTEIN TYPE/CUT OF MEAT	ESTIMATED COOKING TIME	COOKING TEMPERATURE	DONE TEMPERATURE	REST TIME	PREFERRED WOOD
Salmon	3 to 4 hours	180°F	145°F	N/A	Apple, oak, maple, pecan
Scallops	45 minutes to 1 hour	210°F	145°F	N/A	Alder, apple, cherry
Shrimp	30 to 45 minutes	225°F	120°F	N/A	Alder, apple, cherry

		SEAFOOD			
PROTEIN TYPE/CUT OF MEAT	ESTIMATED COOKING TIME	COOKING TEMPERATURE	DONE TEMPERATURE	REST TIME	PREFERRED WOOD
Tilapia	1 to 2 hours	225°F	145°F	N/A	Alder, apple, cherry
Lobster	45 minutes to 1 hour	250°F	140°F	N/A	Apple, cherry
Ahi Tuna	30 to 45 minutes	140°F	125°F	N/A	Apple, cherry
Crab Legs	30 to 45 minutes	225°F	110 to 140°F	N/A	Cherry
Catfish	1 to 2 hours	225°F	145°F	N/A	Alder, apple, cherry
Mahi-Mahi	30 to 45 minutes	225°F	145°F	N/A	Apple, cherry

MEAT SMOKING FAQS

No matter how much you study smoking meat, you'll probably still have questions when it comes to putting it into practice. And that's a good thing. Many readers ask me questions about smoking food. I've combined the most commonly asked questions here in hopes that this information answers questions you may have as well!

Q: When should I add more wood to the smoker?

A: My general rule when using a gas smoker is to check the wood pan every four to five hours and only add more wood when it looks burnt or it has started to turn to ash. If half the pan still has fresh wood, let it keep burning without adding more wood, then check it again in an hour. When you have long smokes (more than six hours), it's important to keep the fire going with fresh wood. Just because the smoker is still smoking doesn't mean the wood is still burning.

Q: When using a gas smoker, about an hour or so into the smoke, the wood chunks catch fire. Why does my wood catch on fire while smoking?

A: The wood is most likely catching on fire because it is being exposed to too much oxygen. I typically see this happen when the door is opened to baste the meat. While basting during the smoking process is okay, try to keep it to a minimum. You want to keep the lid on the smoker closed as much as possible.

To help prevent the wood from catching on fire, try wrapping dry wood chunks in heavy-duty foil. This method limits the amount of oxygen the wood is exposed to. You can also poke holes in the foil to allow some oxygen to enter and smoke to escape. Then, put the foil pouch in the wood pan. This process has helped me when I frequently open the smoker lid to baste the meat. If this doesn't help, try soaking the wood chunks overnight, then put them directly in the wood pan. You can also wrap soaked wood chunks in a foil pouch, just like when treating the dry chunks.

Q: I just bought a smoker. Do I need to season it before my first smoke?

A: Yes, you should always season (or cure) your smoker before the first smoke. And the good thing is, you'll only have to season it once. Seasoning a smoker at high heat burns off any residues left from the manufacturing process. How you season it and for how long depends on the type of smoker you have. Refer to the owner's manual for their recommended instructions.

Q: How do I get my smoker at the right temperature for the amount of time I need to smoke a piece of meat and successfully maintain that temperature?

A: Keeping your fire fueled is key here. If you have a pellet or electric smoker, you have nothing to worry about since it does all temperature regulation for you. For a gas or charcoal smoker, there's a bit more involved. Refer to the Wood and Other Fuel Sources on page 7 and How to Build and Feed Your Fire on page 11 for how to best regulate and maintain temperature.

Q: How do I ensure I don't overpower the meat I'm smoking with too much smoke flavor or not enough smoke?

A: This can happen if you use a wood flavor that is too strong for a certain type of meat. For example, walnut wood is very strong and bitter and will quickly overpower a light and delicate fish like halibut. Refer to either the Meat Smoking Chart on page 22 or the Wood Flavors chart on page 9 for the best wood/meat pairing suggestions and recommendations.

Q: What do you do when the meat stops cooking while in the smoker?

A: This is called a stall and happens when smoking certain types of meats like brisket and pork shoulder. There are a lot of theories as to why stalls happen, and you'll get different answers based on who you ask. The important thing to know is there are several ways to get past the stall. I talk about these methods in my Smoked Brisket recipe (page 84) and Smoked Boston Butt recipe (page 61).

Q: How do I know if I have properly inserted the digital thermometer?

A: Insert the thermometer at a slight angle. When inserting a digital thermometer into the meat, ensure it does not touch any part of the bone. Bone conducts heat faster than meat, which will result in a higher temperature reading.

Q: How do I ensure my meat is done? I don't want to overcook or undercook it.

A: Always use a meat thermometer, preferably a digital one. Never solely rely on a time estimate because if the temperature isn't precisely maintained in the smoker, you could easily overcook or undercook the meat. For the purposes of this cookbook, remove the meat from the smoker at the recommended "done" temperature, even though the temperature may rise several degrees while the meat is resting. Refer to the Done Temperature column in the Meat Smoking Chart on page 22 so you can ensure your meat is smoked to the appropriate and recommended temperature.

Q: When the meat reaches the done temperature, should I reinsert the temperature gauge in a different part of the meat before I remove it from the smoker?

A: Yes, but be careful not to pierce too many holes in the meat. The more you pierce the meat, the more juice will escape. I recommend piercing the thickest part of the meat in at least two different locations on opposite sides.

Q: When smoking baby back ribs, should I leave the membrane on or take it off?

A: There are a lot of opinions out there on this one. It's a personal preference. I always remove the membrane because it helps the meat absorb more of the smoke flavor. Plus, the membrane is tough and harder to chew.

Q: Where is the best place to buy meat?

A: There are a lot of places where you can buy meat for smoking. I've had good results with buying meat at grocery store chains, but I've always had the best results getting it from a butcher instead. If a butcher shop can tell me exactly where the meat comes from, I'll become one of their lifelong customers.

Q: Should I trim the fat off the meat?

A: This depends on the type of meat and how much fat it contains. A lot of people don't trim the fat away; it's a matter of personal preference. For meats like brisket and pork belly, I like to leave about a quarter-inch of fat on the meat before smoking. You can ask a butcher to do this for you, or you can trim the fat yourself.

Q: Can I smoke meat in the same liquid I marinated it in?

A: No. Always discard the marinade to avoid contamination.

Q: How do I know how much gas is left in my propane tank?

A: Here's a quick tip for checking: An empty propane tank weighs somewhere between 17 and 19 pounds. Use a bathroom scale to weigh it; the difference in the numbers is how much gas is left.

Q: If a recipe says the smoking temperature should be at 225°F, is it okay if the internal temperature of the smoker goes a little above or below 225°F?

A: Yes, the internal smoking temperature will always be a range. In this specific case, if you keep the smoker temperature between 225°F and 250°F during the smoking process, you're in good shape. Try to keep it more toward 225°F but not exceeding 250°F.

Q: Should I flip the meat while it's smoking?

A: As a general rule, you don't need to flip meat while it's smoking. The lid should stay closed as much as possible to maintain the internal temperature of the smoker. When the smoker lid is opened, heat escapes and can disrupt the internal temperature. Now, that's not to say you should *never* open the smoker lid. There are some recipes where meat should be repositioned or basted, which requires the lid to be opened—just keep it minimal. When smoking smaller pieces of meat such as chicken breasts or rib eye steaks, you should keep the lid closed for the entire smoking process. Smoking isn't like grilling. In a smoker, the internal temperature must be maintained.

Q: There is a netting over the meat I purchased. Should I remove the netting before smoking or leave it on?

A: You will often see a roast or prime rib come wrapped in netting or twine. As a general rule, if a particular meat has netting in place when purchased, it's best to leave it on while smoking. When meat is cooked, it expands, and the netting is there to ensure that particular cut of meat stays in place during the smoke.

ABOUT THE RECIPES

So, are you ready to jump in and start smoking some meat? Now that you have the basics down, it's time to apply some of what you've learned. To keep things organized and super easy for you, the recipes are divided into chapters based on type of meat. We're going to start with pork recipes, then move into beef and lamb, and, finally, we'll be smoking some poultry and seafood. The very last chapter contains recipes for my most popular rubs, sauces, and marinades that are used in a lot of the recipes in this book. The chapter also features a a handful of my favorite smoked side dish recipes that pair amazingly well with so many of the smoked meat recipes in this book.

As far as equipment goes, most of the recipes will require basic tools like a basting brush and tongs. And to keep things as easy as possible, I've minimized the need for any special equipment.

You don't have to follow the order of each recipe chapter. If you want to start out by smoking chicken or beef, go for it! Along the way, I'll also share some of my expert advice and best secrets I've learned over the years when it comes to certain smoking methods.

As you venture into the world of meat smoking, just remember that even though there is some science to it, smoking is an art—and it's actually pretty easy. You just need to get comfortable with the process.

CHAPTER 2

PORK

Smoked Chorizo Links with Garlic Aioli 38

Smoked Bratwursts with Sauerkraut
and Tarragon Dijon Sauce 39

Candied Barbecue Smoked Bacon 40

Smoked Pit Ham 42

Pineapple-Glazed Smoked Ham 45

Herb Smoked Pork Chops 47

Garlic-Herb Smoked Pork Loin 48

Smoked Boneless Pork Tenderloin 50

Smoked Ham Hocks 52

Kansas City–Style Barbecue Smoked
Pork Belly Burnt Ends 54

St. Louis–Style Smoked Spare Ribs 57

Smoked Baby Back Ribs 59

Smoked Boston Butt 61

I love to smoke pork. Not only does it taste amazing, but it's also super versatile. Did you know that just about every part of the pig can be consumed? Many cuts of pork also tend to be relatively inexpensive. You have lots options in terms of variety when it comes to smoking pork: You can make sausage links, ribs, pork chops, pulled pork, bacon, and so much more.

For a long time, people used to think pork had to be cooked to an internal temperature of 160°F before it could be consumed, which left pork very dry. But in 2011, the USDA published new guidelines stating that pork can safely be cooked to 145°F with a three-minute rest. And let me tell you, that decision made a *world* of difference flavor-wise, especially when it comes to pork chops, loins, and tenderloins.

Pork should be tender, juicy, and full of flavor, and getting it to the right internal temperature when smoking is key. I'm going to cover the most popular cuts and talk about different brine flavors, rubs, and sauces. You'll also discover smoking techniques that can be applied to pork. I'll start with smoking prepackaged sausage links to get you familiar and comfortable with your smoker. Smoking sausage links is easy and low maintenance but extremely delicious. Then, I'll present smoking pork chops, tenderloin, and ribs.

So, let's dive in and start smoking!

Smoked Chorizo Links with Garlic Aioli

**SERVES: 6 TO 8 / PREP TIME: 20 MINUTES / SMOKE TIME: 1 HOUR /
RECOMMENDED WOOD: APPLE**

When it comes to chorizo links, there are a lot of different varieties and flavors to choose from. While you can make your own from scratch, it's much simpler to buy them prepackaged. You can find relatively inexpensive prepackaged chorizo links at your local grocer or butcher. Smoked chorizo links tend to be a little spicy, which is why I like to serve them with my homemade Garlic Aioli. The coolness from the fresh lemon juice and mayonnaise helps temper the spicy flavor.

1 (14- to 16-ounce) package chorizo links (about 6)

¼ cup Garlic Aioli (page 159)

1. Prepare the smoker and preheat until the internal temperature reaches 225°F.

2. Put the links directly on the smoker racks and insert a digital thermometer.

3. When the internal temperature reaches 165°F, remove the chorizo links from the smoker and let rest for 3 minutes.

4. Slice the links and dip them in the garlic aioli.

STORAGE: Store covered in the refrigerator for up to 4 days. To serve, reheat the links in a 350°F oven for 10 minutes or until heated through.

Smoked Bratwursts with Sauerkraut and Tarragon Dijon Sauce

SERVES: **4 TO 6** / PREP TIME: **30 MINUTES** / SMOKE TIME: **2 HOURS** / RECOMMENDED WOOD: **APPLE**

Bratwurst are a fall favorite, but I smoke them year-round. While they are delicious on their own, I prefer to serve them over sauerkraut and topped with a rich and creamy tarragon Dijon sauce. The mustard pairs extremely well with pork, and its creaminess, combined with the unique herbal flavor of tarragon, makes for a perfect pairing. Just like sausage links, you can make your own bratwurst, but it's just easier to buy them prepackaged from your local grocer or butcher.

1 (14- to 16-ounce) package bratwurst links (about 6)

1 (14.5-ounce) can sauerkraut

1 cup Tarragon Dijon Sauce (page 152)

1. Prepare the smoker and preheat until the internal temperature reaches 225°F.

2. Put each bratwurst link directly on the smoker racks and insert a digital thermometer.

3. Smoke for 2 hours, or until the internal temperature reaches 160°F.

4. Make the sauerkraut according to package directions. Cover and set aside.

5. When finished smoking, remove the links from the smoker and let rest for 3 minutes before serving with sauerkraut and tarragon Dijon sauce.

EASY SUBSTITUTION TIP: If you can't find fresh tarragon, use 2 teaspoons of dried tarragon instead.

STORAGE: Store covered in the refrigerator for up to 4 days. To serve, reheat the bratwursts in a 350°F oven for 15 minutes or until heated through.

Candied Barbecue Smoked Bacon

**SERVES: 6 / PREP TIME: 15 MINUTES / SMOKE TIME: 45 MINUTES /
RECOMMENDED WOOD: APPLE OR CHERRY**

I have become addicted to candied bacon, and I make it often for gatherings and get-togethers because it's so easy to make and everyone loves it. When bacon's smoked, it becomes crispy and caramelized.

Dad taught me about curing and making my own bacon from pork belly, but we're keeping it easy with this recipe and using prepackaged thick-cut bacon instead. You can buy it packaged or have the butcher cut it for you. I brush each slice of bacon with my homemade barbecue sauce and then add just enough sweet and spicy seasoning to make the flavor pop. While it's great on its own, I've added this candied bacon to burgers for an additional layer of flavor.

4 tablespoons packed light brown sugar

1 tablespoon smoked paprika

¼ teaspoon freshly ground black pepper

¼ teaspoon cayenne pepper

1 cup Carolina Mustard Barbecue Sauce (page 151)

1 pound pork bacon, sliced thick

1. In a small bowl, combine the brown sugar, paprika, black pepper, and cayenne pepper. Set aside.

2. With a basting brush, apply the barbecue sauce onto both sides of each piece of bacon.

3. Sprinkle 1 teaspoon of dry rub onto one side of each piece of bacon, using the basting brush to spread the mixture evenly. Set aside.

4. Prepare the smoker and preheat until the internal temperature reaches 275°F.

5. Cover a baking sheet with heavy-duty foil. Put a wire rack on top of the baking sheet, and put each piece of bacon, spaced evenly, on the wire rack.

6. Put the baking sheet in the smoker with the bacon seasoned-side up, and smoke for 20 minutes.

7. Using tongs, flip each piece of bacon and sprinkle 1 teaspoon of dry rub on the opposite side of each piece of bacon, using the basting brush to spread the mixture evenly.

8. Continue to smoke the bacon for 25 more minutes and then remove from the smoker.

9. Let rest for 3 minutes and serve.

STORAGE: Candied bacon can be kept in the refrigerator for 3 days. It can be reheated in a skillet over low heat.

Smoked Pit Ham

SERVES: 6 TO 8 / **PREP TIME: 15 MINUTES** / **SMOKE TIME: 3 TO 4 HOURS** /
RECOMMENDED WOOD: APPLE OR CHERRY

Ham isn't just for the holidays—this recipe is delicious all year long. Pressing a dozen whole cloves into the ham provides a subtle spice flavor that tastes amazing with the natural sweetness of the meat. Coated with a mixture of pineapple juice and brown sugar, this ham is moist and full of flavor.

FOR THE BASTE

4 tablespoons (½ stick) salted butter

½ cup pineapple juice

¼ cup packed dark brown sugar

FOR THE HAM

1 (5-pound) pit ham

2 tablespoons yellow mustard

¼ cup packed dark brown sugar

12 whole cloves

TO PREPARE THE BASTE

1. In a small saucepan, melt the butter on the stovetop over medium-low heat.

2. Add the pineapple juice and brown sugar, mixing well to combine.

3. Cover and set aside.

TO SMOKE THE HAM

4. Prepare the smoker and preheat until the internal temperature reaches 250°F.

5. Rub the entire ham with the mustard.

6. Then, rub the brown sugar onto the ham to cover all sides.

7. Press the cloves into the ham by making 3 rows with 4 whole cloves in each row, spread out 1 inch apart.

8. Put the ham directly on the smoker racks and insert a digital thermometer.

9. When the ham reaches an internal temperature of 80°F, baste it with the basting liquid.

10. Baste the ham again when it reaches an internal temperature of 110°F, and again at 135°F.

11. The ham is fully cooked when it reaches an internal temperature of 145°F.

12. Using tongs, remove the ham from the smoker. Let rest uncovered for 5 minutes.

13. Remove the whole cloves and discard. Slice the ham and serve.

STORAGE: Store covered in the refrigerator for up to 4 days. This ham is delicious eaten chilled, but if you prefer to serve it warm, reheat it in a 350°F oven for 15 minutes or until heated through.

Pineapple-Glazed Smoked Ham

SERVES: 12 / **PREP TIME: 20 MINUTES** / **SMOKE TIME: 3 TO 4 HOURS** /
RECOMMENDED WOOD: APPLE OR CHERRY

This ham graces my table every Christmas and Easter. It's easier to make if the ham is whole and not presliced. Since I'm using a fully cooked ham, all that's left to do is add a little more flavor in the form of melted butter and sweet pineapple juice and throw it in the smoker.

FOR THE DRY RUB

½ cup packed light
brown sugar

2 tablespoons
smoked paprika

1 tablespoon garlic powder

½ tablespoon
onion powder

2 teaspoons
mustard powder

½ teaspoon ground cloves

½ tablespoon freshly
ground black pepper

1 tablespoon kosher salt

FOR THE BASTE

½ cup apple cider

½ cup pineapple juice

2 tablespoons unsalted
butter, melted

TO MAKE THE DRY RUB

1. In a small bowl, combine the brown sugar, paprika, garlic powder, onion powder, mustard powder, cloves, pepper, and salt. Set aside.

TO MAKE THE BASTE

2. In a medium microwave-safe bowl, melt the butter.

3. Remove the bowl from the microwave and add the apple cider and pineapple juice.

4. Mix well and then set aside.

TO MAKE THE GLAZE

5. Combine the ingredients for the glaze in a small saucepan.

6. Melt on medium heat, then reduce heat to low and let simmer for 7 to 10 minutes.

7. Remove from the heat and set aside.

TO SMOKE THE HAM

8. Prepare the smoker and preheat until the internal temperature reaches 225°F.

9. Baste the ham with the basting liquid.

10. Cover the ham completely with the dry rub.

CONTINUED ▶

FOR THE GLAZE

2 tablespoons salted butter, melted

½ cup packed light brown sugar

3 tablespoons apple cider

1 tablespoon Dijon mustard

FOR THE HAM

7- to 8-pound bone-in, precooked ham

8 to 10 pineapple slices, fresh or canned

11. Using toothpicks to attach the pineapple rings to the ham, cover the meat's exterior with the fruit. The pineapple rings should not overlap.

12. If the ham is presliced, set it sliced-side down in a disposable aluminum pan. If it's not presliced, set the ham directly on the smoker racks and insert a digital thermometer.

13. Smoke for 1 hour.

14. After 1 hour, baste the ham with the basting liquid.

15. Continue to smoke the ham for another 2 to 3 hours, basting every 45 minutes.

16. The ham is fully cooked when it reaches an internal temperature of 145°F. Using tongs, remove the ham from the smoker.

17. Let rest uncovered for 5 minutes and then serve, topping with glaze.

EASY INGREDIENT TIP: It's easier to make this recipe if the ham isn't presliced. You are able to put the ham directly on the smoker racks, and the pineapple slices, secured with the toothpicks, will stay in position better. If your ham is presliced (typically a quarter of the way through), put the ham sliced-side down in a disposable aluminum pan. Or, use a cooking net or piece of twine to hold the ham in place. Using toothpicks, place the pineapple slices directly above where the slices start.

STORAGE: Store covered in the refrigerator for up to 4 days. To serve warm, reheat it in a 350°F oven for 15 minutes or until heated through.

Herb Smoked Pork Chops

SERVES: 4 / **PREP TIME:** 10 MINUTES (PLUS UP TO 4 HOURS TO MARINATE) /
SMOKE TIME: 45 MINUTES TO 1 HOUR / **RECOMMENDED WOOD:** APPLE

Smoking pork chops takes this staple weeknight dinner to a whole new level. The ingredients in the marinade are savory and taste amazing with pork. Serve the chops with mashed potatoes or macaroni and cheese to finish off the meal.

¼ cup extra-virgin olive oil, divided

4 bone-in pork chops (1½ inches thick)

2 teaspoons kosher salt

1 teaspoon fennel seeds, ground

½ teaspoon freshly ground black pepper

3 garlic cloves, chopped

2 tablespoons chopped fresh rosemary

1 tablespoon chopped fresh parsley

TO PREPARE THE PORK CHOPS

1. Brush 2 tablespoons of olive oil onto each side of the pork chops. Set aside.

2. In a small bowl, mix the remaining 2 tablespoons of olive oil with the salt, fennel seeds, pepper, garlic, rosemary, and parsley. Rub onto all sides of the pork chops.

3. Put the pork chops in a glass dish and cover with plastic wrap. Marinate in the refrigerator up to 4 hours.

TO SMOKE THE PORK CHOPS

4. Prepare the smoker and preheat until the internal temperature reaches 250°F.

5. While the smoker is preheating, remove the pork chops from the refrigerator. Uncover and let rest at room temperature for 10 minutes.

6. Put the pork chops directly onto the smoker racks and insert a digital thermometer.

7. Smoke the pork chops until they reach an internal temperature of 145°F.

8. Using tongs, remove the pork chops from the smoker. Let rest for 3 minutes before serving.

Garlic-Herb Smoked Pork Loin

SERVES: 6 TO 8 / **PREP TIME:** 20 MINUTES (PLUS UP TO 4 HOURS TO BRINE) /
SMOKE TIME: 3 TO 4 HOURS / **RECOMMENDED WOOD:** APPLE OR CHERRY

Let the smoker do all the work with this boneless pork loin! This recipe takes minimal effort to prepare and results in the most succulent piece of meat. When you remove the pork loin from the brine, don't pat it dry—this is the key to maintaining moisture. The pork loin should stay wet when applying the dry rub in order to trap the juices when it's wrapped tightly in foil. This meal is an excellent choice for any weeknight or Sunday dinner, and it pairs well with carrots, potatoes, and green beans.

FOR THE PORK LOIN

1 (5-pound) boneless pork loin

FOR THE BRINE

6 cups cold water

2 cups apple cider vinegar

½ cup packed light brown sugar

¼ cup kosher salt

2 tablespoons whole black peppercorns

2 rosemary sprigs

2 bay leaves

3 garlic cloves, chopped

FOR THE DRY RUB

1 tablespoon kosher salt

½ teaspoon freshly ground black pepper

1 teaspoon dried basil

TO MAKE THE BRINE

1. In a large bowl, combine the water, apple cider vinegar, brown sugar, salt, peppercorns, rosemary, bay leaves, and garlic.

2. Pour the brine into a gallon-size resealable plastic bag, then put the pork loin in the bag and let it marinate for up to 4 hours.

TO MAKE THE DRY RUB

3. In a small bowl, combine the salt, pepper, basil, oregano, thyme, parsley, garlic, and sage.

4. Remove the pork loin from the brine and put it on a cutting board. Remember: Do not pat it dry! The pork loin should remain wet.

5. Rub the pork loin with the olive oil.

6. Apply the dry rub to the pork loin. The pork loin should be very moist.

1 teaspoon dried oregano

1 teaspoon dried thyme

1 teaspoon dried parsley

1 teaspoon garlic powder

¼ teaspoon dried sage

1 tablespoon extra-virgin olive oil

FOR THE WET RUB

4 tablespoons (½ stick) salted butter, at room temperature

10 garlic cloves, chopped

½ teaspoon kosher salt

½ teaspoon freshly ground black pepper

¼ cup chopped fresh parsley

TO SMOKE THE PORK LOIN

7. Prepare the smoker and preheat until the internal temperature reaches 225°F.

8. Put the pork loin directly onto the smoker racks and insert a digital thermometer.

9. In a small bowl, combine the butter, garlic, salt, pepper, and parsley to make the wet rub.

10. When the pork loin reaches an internal temperature of 110°F, use tongs to remove it from the smoker.

11. Using a basting brush, coat the pork loin evenly with the wet rub, then wrap it in heavy-duty foil.

12. Put the pork loin back in the smoker and continue smoking until it reaches an internal temperature of 145°F.

13. Using tongs, remove the wrapped pork loin from the smoker and let rest for 3 minutes before slicing.

EASY PREP TIP: When wrapping the pork loin in heavy-duty foil toward the end of the smoking process, ensure that the shiny side of the foil is touching the meat. This helps hold in more heat while the pork loin continues to smoke. To add extra flavor, the leftover juice from the foil wrapping can be poured over the slices of meat.

Smoked Boneless Pork Tenderloin

SERVES: 6 TO 8 / PREP TIME: 20 MINUTES (PLUS UP TO 4 HOURS TO BRINE) /
SMOKE TIME: 2 TO 3 HOURS / RECOMMENDED WOOD: APPLE OR CHERRY

Brined in a citrus-based liquid and then coated with a flavorful barbecue spice rub, this is a "no-hassle" smoker recipe. The tender and delicious pork tenderloin also makes for great leftovers. It pairs well with rice and pinto beans topped with cheese and lettuce when making tacos or burrito bowls. Or try pork tenderloin in a quesadilla!

FOR THE PORK TENDERLOIN

1 (2-pound) pork tenderloin

St. Louis–Style Barbecue Sauce (page 148)

FOR THE BRINE

1 cup apple cider vinegar

2 cups water

2 tablespoons kosher salt

¼ cup granulated sugar

1 orange, sliced thin

1 lemon, sliced thin

2 teaspoons dried rosemary

2 bay leaves

2 garlic cloves, crushed

TO MAKE THE BRINE

1. In a large bowl, combine the apple cider vinegar, water, salt, sugar, orange slices, lemon slices, rosemary, bay leaves, and garlic.

2. Put the pork loin into a gallon-size resealable plastic bag, then pour the brine in and let it marinate for up to 4 hours.

TO MAKE THE DRY RUB

3. After the pork has brined, remove it from the bag and put it on a cutting board. Do not pat it dry. The tenderloin should remain wet.

4. In a small bowl, combine the brown sugar, salt, pepper, paprika, onion powder, and garlic powder.

5. Completely cover the pork tenderloin with the dry rub.

TO SMOKE THE PORK TENDERLOIN

6. Prepare the smoker and preheat until the internal temperature reaches 225°F.

7. Put the tenderloin directly on the smoker racks and insert a digital thermometer.

3 tablespoons packed light brown sugar

1 teaspoon kosher salt

1 teaspoon freshly ground black pepper

2 teaspoons smoked paprika

1 teaspoon onion powder

1 teaspoon garlic powder

8. Smoke for 1 hour; using tongs, remove the tenderloin from the smoker and baste on both sides with the barbecue sauce.

9. Continue to smoke the tenderloin until the internal temperature reaches 145°F.

10. Using tongs, remove the tenderloin from the smoker.

11. Let rest uncovered for 3 minutes. Slice the tenderloin and serve immediately.

STORAGE: Store covered in the refrigerator for up to 4 days. To serve, reheat it in a 350°F oven for 10 minutes or until heated through.

Smoked Ham Hocks

SERVES: 4 TO 6 / **PREP TIME:** 10 MINUTES (PLUS 4 HOURS TO BRINE) /
SMOKE TIME: 2 HOURS / **RECOMMENDED WOOD:** HICKORY OR APPLE

If you've never had a soup, turnip greens, or a pot of homemade beans flavored with smoked ham hock, you're missing out! Ham hock naturally provides a ton of flavor to food, but smoking it takes things to a whole new level. With this recipe, you'll want to brine the ham hocks for at least 4 hours. Then, you'll smoke them on a low temperature for a couple of hours. And that's it!

FOR THE BRINE

7 cups water

¾ cup kosher salt

½ cup packed dark brown sugar

1 teaspoon whole black peppercorns

FOR THE HAM

2 ham hocks

TO MAKE THE BRINE

1. In a large bowl, combine the water, salt, brown sugar, and peppercorns.

2. Put the ham hocks in a gallon-size resealable plastic bag.

3. Pour the brine into the bag with the ham hocks and seal.

4. Put the bag into a large bowl to catch any liquid that may leak during the brining process.

5. Refrigerate for at least 4 hours.

6. Once done, remove the ham hocks from the brine and dry each piece with a paper towel to remove any excess water; this helps the meat absorb as much smoke as possible, which adds to the flavor.

TO SMOKE THE HAM HOCKS

7. Prepare the smoker and preheat until the internal temperature reaches 200°F.

8. Put the ham hocks directly on the smoker racks and smoke for 2 hours, until they reach an internal temperature of 150°F.

9. Using tongs, remove the ham hocks from the smoker.

10. Put them uncovered on a cooling rack.

11. Once completely cooled, the smoked ham hocks are ready for use.

EASY PREP TIP: When you're ready to use the smoked ham hocks, use a knife or kitchen shears to cut through the skin and cartilage and remove the meat. Then, chop the meat into bite-size pieces and use in soups, beans, etc.

STORAGE: Refrigerate the smoked ham hocks for up to 5 days. Or freeze all the ham hocks in a plastic bag for later use. The ham hocks should last in the freezer for up to 6 months.

Kansas City–Style Barbecue Smoked Pork Belly Burnt Ends

SERVES: 4 TO 5 / **PREP TIME:** 20 MINUTES / **SMOKE TIME:** 4 TO 5 HOURS / **RECOMMENDED WOOD:** APPLE OR CHERRY

Pork belly burnt ends are made from the same cut as bacon, so there's a reason they're called meat candy! Juicy and tender, these burnt ends are perfect as an appetizer or as an entree. For this recipe, you'll need a barbecue grilling basket.

FOR THE PORK BELLY

1 (5-pound) pork belly

3 tablespoons yellow mustard

¼ cup packed dark brown sugar

2 tablespoons kosher salt

1 tablespoon freshly ground black pepper

1 tablespoon smoked paprika

1 teaspoon chili powder

1 teaspoon garlic powder

½ teaspoon onion powder

½ teaspoon ground cumin

FOR THE SAUCE

1 cup Kansas City–Style Barbecue Sauce (page 150)

4 tablespoons (½ stick) salted butter, sliced

3 tablespoons honey

TO MAKE THE PORK BELLY

1. With a pair of kitchen shears or a sharp knife, trim off any excess fat from the pork, leaving a thin layer in place.

2. Using a basting brush, completely cover the pork with the mustard.

3. In a small bowl, combine the brown sugar, salt, pepper, paprika, chili powder, garlic powder, onion powder, and cumin. Set aside.

4. With a sharp knife, cut the pork belly into 1½-inch cubes.

5. Cover the pork belly pieces completely with the dry rub.

6. Put the pork belly cubes in a barbecue grilling basket.

TO SMOKE THE PORK BELLY

7. Prepare the smoker and preheat until the internal temperature reaches 250°F.

8. Put the barbecue grilling basket in the smoker and smoke for 3 hours.

9. After 3 hours, remove the pork belly burnt ends from the smoker.

10. Put the burnt ends into a disposable aluminum pan.

11. Add the barbecue sauce, butter, and honey and stir to coat evenly.

12. Insert a digital thermometer into a pork belly cube and cover the pan with foil, then put the pan back into the smoker.

13. When the internal temperature reaches 205°F, remove the foil from the pan using tongs and continue smoking uncovered for an additional 10 to 15 minutes.

14. Using oven mitts, remove the burnt ends from the smoker.

15. Let rest for 7 to 10 minutes, then top with more barbecue sauce and serve.

EASY FLAVOR BOOST: While you can use any of my homemade barbecue sauces in this book on burnt ends, my favorite is this Kansas City–style barbecue sauce. The sweet and spicy layered flavors in the sauce mixed with the dry rub provides amazing flavor!

St. Louis–Style Smoked Spare Ribs

SERVES: 4 / **PREP TIME:** 20 MINUTES / **SMOKE TIME:** 4 TO 5 HOURS /
RECOMMENDED WOOD: **APPLE, CHERRY, OR PECAN**

Spare ribs tend to be a bit tougher than baby back ribs, but that doesn't mean they can't be juicy and tender. This is my son's all-time favorite smoker recipe. Davis isn't a huge fan of meat to begin with, but he loves these barbecue pork spare ribs and can eat half a rack all by himself! They are messy but very tender and have an amazing smoky flavor in every bite.

FOR THE RIBS

1 full rack (3 to 4 pounds) spare ribs

2 tablespoons extra-virgin olive oil

1 cup St. Louis–Style Barbecue Sauce, divided (page 148)

FOR THE DRY RUB

½ cup packed light brown sugar

2 tablespoons smoked paprika

1 teaspoon onion powder

1 teaspoon celery seed

1 teaspoon garlic powder

1 teaspoon kosher salt

1 teaspoon white pepper

TO PREPARE THE RIBS

1. Trim any excess fat from the ribs and remove the membrane on the back, or have the butcher do this for you.

2. Brush the spare ribs with the olive oil.

TO PREPARE THE DRY RUB

3. In a small bowl, combine the brown sugar, paprika, onion powder, celery seed, garlic powder, salt, and pepper.

4. Cover the ribs completely with the dry rub.

TO SMOKE THE RIBS

5. Prepare the smoker and preheat until the internal temperature reaches 225°F.

6. Put the ribs directly on the smoker racks and let them smoke for 3 hours.

7. After 3 hours, remove the ribs from the smoker using a pair of tongs.

8. On a piece of heavy-duty foil, brush the ribs with ½ cup of barbecue sauce.

CONTINUED ▸

9. Tightly wrap the ribs in the foil and put them back in the smoker until the internal temperature reaches 203°F.

10. Using tongs, remove the ribs from the smoker and let rest for 10 minutes.

11. Remove the foil and baste the ribs with the remaining ½ cup of barbecue sauce with a clean basting brush. Serve immediately.

EASY PREP TIP: To remove the membrane from the ribs, you'll first need to loosen it. Find the thin translucent-white layer of tissue that is attached to the ribs. With a small butter knife, raise a corner of the membrane, which should be at the edge of the ribs. Slide the knife under it and remove it with your fingers by pulling up and out.

Smoked Baby Back Ribs

**SERVES: 4 TO 6 / PREP TIME: 20 MINUTES / SMOKE TIME: 5 TO 6 HOURS /
RECOMMENDED WOOD: APPLE OR CHERRY**

Every time I light the smoker, my daughter Kyliegh asks if I'm smoking baby back ribs. This recipe is her favorite, and she requests smoked baby back ribs every year for her birthday. A summertime staple, baby back ribs are known for being so incredibly tender that the rib meat falls right off the bone. Just remember to remove the membrane before smoking. To do so, find the thin translucent-white layer of tissue. Slide a small butter knife under the membrane and remove it with your fingers by pulling up and out. (You can also have a butcher do this for you.)

FOR THE DRY RUB

2 tablespoons packed dark brown sugar

1 tablespoon smoked paprika

1 tablespoon chili powder

¾ teaspoon garlic powder

½ teaspoon freshly ground black pepper

1 teaspoon kosher salt

1 teaspoon dry mustard

FOR THE RIBS

2 (6- to 7-pound) racks of baby back ribs

2 tablespoons extra-virgin olive oil

1½ cups Homestyle Barbecue Sauce, divided (page 147)

TO PREPARE THE DRY RUB

1. In a small bowl, combine the brown sugar, paprika, chili powder, garlic powder, pepper, salt, and dry mustard. Set aside.

TO PREPARE THE RIBS

2. Trim the ribs of any excess fat and remove the membrane, or have the butcher do this for you.

3. Brush the ribs with the olive oil.

4. Prepare the smoker and preheat until the internal temperature reaches 225°F.

5. Cover each slab of ribs completely with the dry rub.

6. Put each slab directly on the smoker racks, bone-side down.

7. Using a basting brush, coat the ribs with ½ cup of barbecue sauce.

8. Smoke at 225°F degrees for 2 hours.

CONTINUED ▶

9. After 2 hours, using a pair of tongs, take the ribs out of the smoker and put them on the shiny side of a large piece of heavy-duty foil.

10. Apply another ½ cup of barbecue sauce on both sides of the ribs.

11. Wrap each slab of ribs individually and tightly inside the foil.

12. Put the ribs back in the smoker, bone-side up, and smoke for 2 more hours.

13. After 2 hours, use a pair of tongs to remove the foil-wrapped ribs from the smoker.

14. Unwrap the ribs and apply the final ½ cup of barbecue sauce using a clean basting brush.

15. Put the ribs back on the smoker uncovered, bone-side down, for 1 more hour.

16. Once done, use tongs to remove the ribs from the smoker and let rest for 10 minutes. Serve with additional barbecue sauce as desired.

EASY PREP TIP: In the last hour of smoking, if the ribs are already starting to fall off the bone, instead of placing them directly on the smoker racks, wrap them in heavy-duty foil and smoke for 1 more hour.

Smoked Boston Butt

SERVES: **6 TO 8** / **PREP TIME:** **20 MINUTES (PLUS UP TO 4 HOURS TO MARINATE)** /
SMOKE TIME: **10 TO 12 HOURS** / **RECOMMENDED WOOD:** **APPLE OR CHERRY**

The terms "pork butt" or "Boston butt" refer to a cut of pork that comes from the upper part of the shoulder. This is my dad's recipe and it has been in our family for decades. I use a bone-in pork shoulder, and when it has finished smoking, the bone literally slides right out. This is the perfect recipe for barbecue sandwiches, tacos, or a pulled pork dinner!

The secret to juicy and tender pulled pork involves several methods. I always spray the pork with apple juice to add flavor, and I also add apple cider vinegar to the water pan to help enhance the flavor of the meat.

1 (8- to 10-pound) pork shoulder

¼ cup yellow mustard

½ cup Boston Butt Rub (page 155)

¼ cup apple juice

¼ cup water

1. Put the pork shoulder on a large baking sheet or in a glass dish. Baste the entire pork shoulder with the mustard until it's coated evenly.

2. Apply the rub to the pork shoulder on all sides until it is completely covered.

3. Cover the glass dish with plastic wrap and put it in the refrigerator to marinate for up to 4 hours.

4. Once marinated, take the pork out of the refrigerator to rest while you prepare the smoker.

5. Preheat the smoker until the internal temperature reaches 225°F.

6. Put the pork directly on the smoker racks, fat-side up, and insert a digital thermometer.

7. When the internal temperature of the pork reaches 165°F, about 2 to 3 hours, remove it from the smoker and put it on a large piece of heavy-duty foil, shiny-side up.

CONTINUED ▶

IF USING A GAS OR CHARCOAL SMOKER:

Check the wood pan every 4 to 5 hours and add more chunks when needed. For this recipe I soak the wood chunks overnight, wrap them in heavy-duty foil before placing in the wood pan, and poke holes in the foil to allow smoke to escape. I typically only have to add to my wood pan once with this recipe.

Mix in 1 cup of apple cider vinegar with 8 to 10 cups of water and pour into the smoker water pan. If using a pellet or electric smoker, use the same ratio of apple cider vinegar and water, pour into a disposable aluminum pan, and put it beside the meat directly on the smoker racks.

8. Pour the apple juice and water into a spray bottle. Spray the meat 4 to 5 times. (This adds flavor and increases the moisture level while the pork continues to smoke.)

9. Tightly wrap the pork shoulder in the heavy-duty foil, and then wrap it again in another piece of foil so the pork is double wrapped.

10. Put the pork back in the smoker and reinsert the digital thermometer.

11. When the internal temperature reaches 203°F, about 3 hours, remove the wrapped pork from the smoker and put it on the counter.

12. Keep the pork wrapped in the foil. Take a large towel and wrap the pork tightly around the foil. This is an important step that traps as much heat as possible while the pork shoulder rests.

13. Put the wrapped meat in an empty cooler and close the lid for 1 hour. The goal is to trap as much heat as possible in a controlled environment while the pork slowly cools.

14. After an hour, remove the pork from the cooler and slowly unwrap the meat. At this point in the process, the meat is done and ready to be shredded.

15. Put the smoked pork butt in a deep pan or glass dish. Pull out the bone and discard.

16. Shred the pork with a pair of meat shredder claws (or 2 forks). The meat should be extremely tender and shred easily. Discard any visible fat while shredding. Add barbecue sauce if desired and serve.

CHAPTER 3

BEEF & LAMB

Smoked Marinated Flank Steak 66

Smoked Mediterranean Lamb Burgers 67

Peppercorn-Crusted Beef Sirloin Tip Roast 68

Montreal Rib Eye 69

Garlic-Rosemary Smoked Lamb Chops 71

Garlic-Crusted Smoked Rack of Lamb 72

Smoked Prime Rib 73

Filet Mignon & Veggie Kebabs 75

Santa Maria–Style Smoked Tri-Tip Steak 77

Smoked Lamb Shoulder with Au Jus 78

Five-Spice Beef Short Ribs 80

Sweet and Spicy Cheese-Stuffed Smoked Meatloaf 82

Smoked Brisket 84

Smoked Brisket Burnt Ends with
Cherry Barbecue Sauce 86

Smoked Chuck Roast 88

With these beef smoker recipes, you can expect tender, juicy, and amazingly flavorful results like you've never tasted before. In this chapter, we'll be smoking different cuts of steak such as rib eye, sirloin, and prime rib as well as a chuck roast, beef short ribs, and even a meatloaf! The chuck roast is one of my favorite recipes in this chapter—I have to say, I never thought smoking a chuck roast could be so flavorful. The same holds true with my smoked flank steak recipe. When smoked, flank steak becomes a surprisingly tender and delicious cut of meat.

This chapter also includes smoked lamb recipes. In certain countries, lamb is a delicacy and the meat of choice. It's extremely versatile and can be paired with so many different spices, foods, and flavors. Smoking lamb may sound intimidating at first, but it's easy to do and is highly forgiving. While lamb tends to have a "gamey" flavor, the smoking process reduces that and balances out the taste with the wood flavors and seasonings used.

As a general note, some recipes in this chapter call for a short marinating time not exceeding four hours. There's some truth behind the thought that the longer the marinate time, the more flavorful the outcome. But for these recipes, I find that a maximum of four hours is a good amount of time for the meat to absorb the flavor from the marinade.

Smoked Marinated Flank Steak

SERVES: 4 TO 6 / **PREP TIME:** 20 MINUTES (PLUS UP TO 4 HOURS TO MARINATE) /
SMOKE TIME: 2 TO 3 HOURS / **RECOMMENDED WOOD:** OAK OR MESQUITE

Flank is naturally a tougher piece of meat because it comes from the abdomen area of the cow, but when you smoke it low and slow, it becomes ridiculously tender. Made with my go-to marinade, this recipe is perfect for any weeknight dinner or cookout with friends.

½ cup extra-virgin olive oil

⅓ cup soy sauce

¼ cup red wine vinegar

2 tablespoons freshly squeezed lemon juice

1½ tablespoons Worcestershire sauce

1 tablespoon Dijon mustard

2 garlic cloves, minced

½ teaspoon freshly ground black pepper

1 (2-pound) flank steak

1. In a medium bowl, combine the olive oil, soy sauce, red wine vinegar, lemon juice, Worcestershire sauce, mustard, garlic, and pepper.

2. Put the steak in a gallon-size resealable plastic bag, then pour in the marinade. Move the liquid around to ensure the steak is well covered.

3. Refrigerate and let it marinate for up to 4 hours.

4. Prepare the smoker and preheat until the internal temperature reaches 225°F.

5. After the steak has marinated, remove it from the plastic bag and let rest on a plate for 10 minutes. Discard the marinade.

6. Put the steak directly on the smoker racks and insert a digital thermometer.

7. Smoke to desired doneness (check Meat Smoking Chart on page 22).

8. Remove the steak from the smoker and let rest for 3 minutes before slicing and serving.

EASY SERVING TIP: I recommend slicing this steak in thin pieces. When slicing, ensure you cut against the grain for maximum tenderness.

Smoked Mediterranean Lamb Burgers

SERVES: 6 / PREP TIME: 30 MINUTES / SMOKE TIME: 45 MINUTES TO 1 HOUR / RECOMMENDED WOOD: APPLE OR OAK

Hamburgers are a tried-and-true family favorite, but have you ever tried a lamb burger—or a smoked one at that? Made with ground lamb, these burgers are exploding with Mediterranean flavor from the fresh rosemary, cumin, parsley, and feta. Instead of adding mayonnaise, top this burger with my Garlic Aioli (page 159). It provides the perfect balance and evens out any gamey flavor from the lamb.

2 pounds ground lamb

½ cup panko bread crumbs

1 tablespoon Worcestershire sauce

2 large eggs, lightly beaten

½ cup feta cheese, crumbled

¼ cup finely chopped red onion

1 tablespoon chopped fresh rosemary

2 tablespoons chopped fresh parsley

¼ teaspoon ground cumin

1 teaspoon kosher salt

½ teaspoon freshly ground black pepper

⅓ cup packed light brown sugar

2 tablespoons smoked paprika

1 tablespoon onion powder

1 tablespoon garlic powder

1. In a large bowl, combine the lamb, bread crumbs, Worcestershire sauce, eggs, cheese, onion, rosemary, parsley, cumin, salt, pepper, brown sugar, paprika, onion powder, and garlic powder with your hands until mixed completely.

2. Take ¼ cup of the lamb mixture and use your hands to press it into the shape of a patty. Repeat with the remaining mixture. Each patty should be around ¾-inch thick.

3. Prepare the smoker and preheat until the internal temperature reaches 250°F.

4. Put each lamb burger patty directly on the smoker racks.

5. After 20 minutes, flip the patties over with a spatula. Insert a digital thermometer into one of the patties.

6. When the internal temperature reaches 165°F, remove the lamb burgers from the smoker and let rest for 3 minutes before serving.

EASY PREP TIP: I use a large round cookie cutter to form the patties; it helps them keep their shape after they've been smoked.

Peppercorn-Crusted Beef Sirloin Tip Roast

**SERVES: 5 TO 6 / PREP TIME: 10 MINUTES / SMOKE TIME: 2 TO 3 HOURS /
RECOMMENDED WOOD: HICKORY OR MESQUITE**

If you enjoy the taste and heat of black pepper, then you'll love this smoked beef sirloin. Instead of smoking individual sirloin steaks, I smoke the entire tip roast so that it forms a peppery bark. The butter and salt are the main players that form this delicious coating. Using crushed peppercorns adds to the texture and taste of this steak, and the white pepper gives it even more bite.

1 tablespoon dried oregano

1 (4-pound) sirloin tip roast

2 tablespoons unsalted butter, at room temperature

2 tablespoons House Seasoning (page 154)

2 teaspoons crushed black peppercorns

¼ teaspoon white pepper

1. Rub the entire sirloin tip roast with the butter.

2. Sprinkle on the house seasoning until roast is evenly coated.

3. Sprinkle on the crushed peppercorns and white pepper.

4. Prepare the smoker and preheat until the internal temperature reaches 250°F.

5. Put the roast directly on the smoker racks and insert a digital thermometer.

6. Smoke for 2 to 3 hours or until desired doneness, then remove the roast from the smoker and let rest for 3 minutes before slicing and serving.

EASY SERVING TIP: When slicing sirloin tip roast, ensure you cut against the grain to maximize the tenderness of the steak.

Montreal Rib Eye

**SERVES: 5 TO 6 / PREP TIME: 10 MINUTES / SMOKE TIME: 2 TO 3 HOURS /
RECOMMENDED WOOD: HICKORY OR MESQUITE**

Rib eye is a premium cut of meat. To be considered a rib eye, the steak must be cut before the roast is cooked. The cuts are then sold as rib eye steaks. My homemade Montreal Dry Rub is perfect for any steak, but I especially love it on a rib eye cut.

⅓ cup Montreal Dry Rub (page 156)

1 (4-pound) boneless rib eye steak

1. Generously apply the rub to the boneless rib eye, pressing firmly into the steak.

2. Prepare the smoker and preheat until the internal temperature reaches 225°F.

3. Put the rib eye steak directly onto the smoking rack and insert a digital thermometer.

4. Smoke for 2 to 3 hours or until desired doneness, then remove the steak from the smoker and let rest for 3 minutes before slicing and serving.

STORAGE: Store covered in the refrigerator for up to 3 days. To serve, reheat in a 350°F oven for 10-15 minutes or until heated through.

Garlic-Rosemary Smoked Lamb Chops

SERVES: 4 / PREP TIME: 20 MINUTES (PLUS 4 HOURS TO MARINATE) /
SMOKE TIME: 1 TO 2 HOURS / **RECOMMENDED WOOD:** APPLE OR CHERRY

If you like pork chops, you'll love these lamb chops! Lamb is naturally tender, but when smoked, it becomes even more tender. While I love the flavor of lamb on its own, the marinade makes this recipe memorable. Pureed fresh ingredients like lime and cilantro with classic Mediterranean spices like rosemary and garlic bring out the savory taste. Lamb chops are quick to smoke and make for an amazing dinner any night of the week!

¼ cup extra-virgin olive oil

6 garlic cloves, chopped

¼ cup onion, chopped

¾ teaspoon kosher salt

½ teaspoon ground cumin

¼ cup chopped fresh cilantro

1 oregano sprig

3 rosemary sprig

1 thyme sprig

¼ teaspoon white pepper

Grated zest and juice of 1 lime

4 to 6 (¾-inch thick) lamb chops (about 2 pounds)

1. Combine the olive oil, garlic, onion, salt, cumin, cilantro, oregano, rosemary, thyme, pepper, and lime juice in a blender or food processor. Puree until well combined.

2. Put the lamb chops into a gallon-size resealable plastic bag. Pour in the marinade and make sure it completely covers the lamb chops, then seal the bag.

3. Marinate in the refrigerator for up to 4 hours.

4. Prepare the smoker and preheat until the internal temperature reaches 225°F.

5. Put the lamb chops directly on the smoker racks and insert a digital thermometer.

6. Smoke for 1 to 2 hours or until desired doneness.

7. Remove the lamb chops from the smoker and let rest for 3 minutes before serving.

EASY SERVING TIP: These lamb chops pair well with my Tzatziki Sauce (page 158) and my Garlic Aioli (page 159). My Tarragon Dijon Sauce (page 152) is also great served on top of lamb chops.

Garlic-Crusted Smoked Rack of Lamb

**SERVES: 4 / PREP TIME: 30 MINUTES / SMOKE TIME: 1 TO 2 HOURS /
RECOMMENDED WOOD: APPLE OR CHERRY**

Let's be honest—rack of lamb can be expensive, but it's such an elegant cut of meat. Although rack of lamb is incredibly flavorful by itself, I add a garlic crust made with fresh herbs and bread crumbs that makes it even more appetizing with every bite. I enjoy eating rack of lamb when it's cooked to an internal temperature of 130°F, which is medium-rare (see page 27 for a meat doneness chart).

½ cup panko bread crumbs

8 garlic cloves, minced

2 tablespoons chopped fresh rosemary

1 teaspoon kosher salt

1 teaspoon freshly ground black pepper

1 teaspoon dried parsley

⅓ cup extra-virgin olive oil

1 (2-pound) rack of lamb

1. In a small bowl, combine the bread crumbs, garlic, rosemary, salt, pepper, and parsley. Set aside.

2. Baste the rack of lamb with the olive oil, then apply the bread crumb mixture pressing it firmly into the meat.

3. Prepare the smoker and preheat until the internal temperature reaches 225°F.

4. Put the rack of lamb directly on the smoker racks, bone-side down, and insert a digital thermometer.

5. Smoke for 1 to 2 hours or until desired doneness.

6. Remove the rack of lamb from the smoker and let rest for 5 minutes before slicing and serving.

EASY PREP TIP: To keep the bones from burning during the smoking process, cover them with heavy-duty foil.

Smoked Prime Rib

**SERVES: 6 TO 7 / PREP TIME: 10 MINUTES / SMOKE TIME: 4 TO 5 HOURS /
RECOMMENDED WOOD: APPLE OR CHERRY**

When it comes to buying prime rib, I only buy from a butcher and only buy prime rib roast, not individual steaks. Prime rib is the highest-quality grade of meat from the cow. It's heavily marbled, tender, and full of flavor. It's very easy to smoke and takes almost no effort at all! Simply apply the rub, insert the digital thermometer, and let it smoke low and slow. I enjoy prime rib most when it's smoked to a medium-rare temperature. To cook it up more after the smoke, just add additional au jus to each individual steak. Au jus is the hot juice that comes out of the steak, so make sure you're slicing the steak on a surface that can capture this liquid.

3 tablespoons freshly ground black pepper

3 tablespoons kosher salt

2 tablespoons granulated garlic

1 tablespoon dried rosemary

2 teaspoons dried oregano

2 teaspoons dried thyme

2 teaspoons smoked paprika

1 teaspoon celery seed

1 teaspoon garlic powder

1 (7- to 8-pound) boneless prime rib

¼ cup extra-virgin olive oil

1. In a small bowl, combine the pepper, salt, granulated garlic, rosemary, oregano, thyme, paprika, celery seed, and garlic powder.

2. Brush the olive oil on the prime rib roast.

3. Completely cover the prime rib with the dry rub.

4. Prepare the smoker and preheat until the internal temperature reaches 225°F.

5. Put the prime rib directly on the smoker racks and insert a digital thermometer.

6. Smoke for 4 to 5 hours or until desired doneness.

7. Remove the steak from the smoker and let rest for 3 minutes before slicing and serving.

EASY INGREDIENT TIP: Prime rib takes about 30 minutes per pound to smoke. Any leftover prime rib is excellent for sandwiches or over a salad.

Filet Mignon & Veggie Kebabs

SERVES: 6 / **PREP TIME:** 30 MINUTES (PLUS UP TO 4 HOURS TO MARINATE) /
SMOKE TIME: 1 TO 2 HOURS / **RECOMMENDED WOOD:** APPLE OR OAK

I love kebabs in the summertime! A popular way to make them is on the grill using sirloin steak. But I like to smoke my kebabs using filet mignon. It's a prime cut of beef that becomes even more tender when smoked low and slow. And kebabs are so versatile! Using a variety of bite-size fruits and vegetables, you can personalize your dinner experience. And if you have leftovers, they are great served on top of a bed of rice for a quick and hearty meal.

FOR THE KEBABS

1 yellow bell pepper, cut in 2-inch chunks

1 red bell pepper, cut in 2-inch chunks

1 green bell pepper, cut in 2-inch chunks

1 sweet onion, cut in 2-inch chunks

1 pineapple, cut in 2-inch chunks

10 to 12 whole mushrooms

10 to 12 cherry tomatoes

2 pounds filet mignon, cut in 1¼-inch chunks

10 to 15 wooden skewers soaked in water for at least one hour

TO PREPARE THE KEBABS

1. Rinse the bell peppers, onion, pineapple, mushrooms, and cherry tomatoes in a colander.

2. Put the cut meat and fruit and vegetables into a gallon-size resealable plastic bag.

TO MAKE THE MARINADE

3. Add the olive oil, soy sauce, lemon juice, red wine vinegar, Worcestershire sauce, Montreal seasoning garlic, and parsley to a blender or food processor and puree until well combined.

4. Pour the marinade into the bag with the steak, fruit, and vegetables and seal.

5. Move the marinade around until it covers all the meat and vegetables. Marinate in the refrigerator for up to 4 hours.

CONTINUED ▶

FOR THE MARINADE

¼ cup extra-virgin olive oil

¼ cup soy sauce

2 tablespoons freshly squeezed lemon juice

2 tablespoons red wine vinegar

1 tablespoon Worcestershire sauce

2 tablespoons Montreal Dry Rub (page 156)

4 garlic cloves

¼ cup fresh parsley

TO SMOKE

6. Prepare the smoker and preheat until the internal temperature reaches 225°F. Remove the steak, fruit, and vegetables from the bag and discard the marinade.

7. To assemble the kebabs, alternate the filet mignon, fruit, and vegetables onto each wooden skewer. Repeat until all steak, fruit, and vegetables are skewered.

8. Put each kebab directly on the smoker racks and insert a digital thermometer into a piece of filet mignon.

9. Smoke for 1 to 2 hours, or until desired doneness, turning each kebab once halfway through.

10. Using tongs, remove the kebabs from the smoker and let rest for 3 minutes before serving.

STORAGE: Store covered in the refrigerator for up to 3 days. To serve, reheat the kebabs in a 350°F oven for 15 minutes or until heated through.

Santa Maria–Style Smoked Tri-Tip Steak

SERVES: 4 TO 5 / PREP TIME: 10 MINUTES / SMOKE TIME: 3 TO 4 HOURS / RECOMMENDED WOOD: OAK OR MESQUITE

Tri-tip is a tender, mild cut of meat shaped like a triangle. It's also called a bottom sirloin butt because it's taken from the sirloin area. It got its name because a butcher from Santa Maria, California, perfected the recipe with a trifecta of sea salt, pepper, and garlic salt. Today, a Santa Maria–style rub has salt, pepper, and either a garlic salt or garlic powder base. When smoking tri-tip, I like to add fresh minced garlic before applying the dry rub to give it even more flavor.

1 teaspoon sea salt

1 teaspoon freshly ground black pepper

½ teaspoon ground cumin

½ teaspoon garlic powder

1 teaspoon smoked paprika

½ teaspoon onion powder

2 tablespoons extra-virgin olive oil

6 garlic cloves, minced

1 (5-pound) tri-tip steak

1. In a small bowl, combine the salt, pepper, cumin, garlic powder, paprika, and onion powder.

2. In a separate small bowl, combine the olive oil with the garlic.

3. Using a basting brush, apply the oil mixture onto both sides of the steak, then cover the steak with the dry rub.

4. Prepare the smoker and preheat until the internal temperature reaches 250°F.

5. Put the steak directly on the smoker racks and insert a digital thermometer.

6. Smoke for 3 to 4 hours or until desired doneness.

7. Remove the steak from the smoker and let rest for 3 minutes before slicing and serving.

EASY SERVING TIP: When slicing, ensure you cut against the grain to maximize the tenderness.

Smoked Lamb Shoulder with Au Jus

**SERVES: 6 TO 8 / PREP TIME: 20 MINUTES / SMOKE TIME: 5 TO 6 HOURS /
RECOMMENDED WOOD: APPLE OR CHERRY**

Lamb shoulder is the perfect dinner recipe to feed a crowd. This smoked lamb has a rich herb-based flavor that's filled with fresh Greek flare. Topped with a vinaigrette-based au jus, this juiciest, most incredible lamb roast pairs well with potatoes and roasted vegetables. If you have any leftovers, it's great in a tortilla wrap with vegetables and lettuce. It can also be added to soups for additional protein.

FOR THE WET RUB

½ cup extra-virgin olive oil

8 garlic cloves, minced

1 tablespoon kosher salt

½ tablespoon freshly ground black pepper

1 tablespoon chopped fresh oregano

2 teaspoons chopped fresh thyme

3 tablespoons chopped fresh rosemary

2 teaspoons chopped fresh sage

TO MAKE THE WET RUB

1. In a small bowl, combine the olive oil, garlic, salt, pepper, oregano, thyme, rosemary, and sage. Set aside.

TO MAKE THE LAMB SHOULDER WITH AU JUS

2. Generously apply the wet rub to the lamb shoulder.

3. Prepare the smoker and preheat until the internal temperature reaches 225°F.

4. Put the lamb shoulder directly on the smoker racks and insert a digital thermometer. You'll need to collect the fat drippings for the au jus, so put a disposable aluminum pan underneath the meat being smoked.

5. Smoke for 4 to 5 hours or to the desired doneness.

6. Remove the lamb shoulder from the smoker and let rest for 10 minutes before slicing. When you slice the finished shoulder, cut off any fatty sections (there won't be many) to add to the au jus as well.

**1 (5-pound) boneless lamb
shoulder**

**2 tablespoons balsamic
vinaigrette**

2 cups beef broth

**1 tablespoon cold
unsalted butter**

1 cinnamon stick

**½ teaspoon packed dark
brown sugar**

7. In a saucepan, bring to a boil the pan drippings, any fatty sections from the lamb, the balsamic vinaigrette, beef broth, butter, cinnamon stick, and brown sugar, then simmer for 30 minutes on low.

8. Discard the cinnamon stick and pour the au jus over the lamb shoulder before serving.

EASY SMOKING TIP: If using a pellet or an electric smoker, put the meat on a wire rack that sits inside a disposable aluminum pan and collect the fat drippings that way.

Five-Spice Beef Short Ribs

**SERVES: 4 / PREP TIME: 20 MINUTES (PLUS UP TO 4 HOURS TO MARINATE) /
SMOKE TIME: 4 TO 5 HOURS / RECOMMENDED WOOD: APPLE OR CHERRY**

These beef short ribs are the perfect comfort food. They're savory, delicious, and smoked to perfection with a rich, dark crust that's full of sweet and spicy flavor. Short ribs don't typically fall off the bone or shred easily, so you'll want to use a sharp knife to slice the meat into thin layers and serve over a bed of jasmine rice or mashed potatoes. I top off this recipe with my signature Cherry Barbecue Sauce, which goes great with the hint of fresh ginger and red pepper flakes in the marinade.

FOR THE MARINADE

4 tablespoons molasses

2 tablespoons soy sauce

1 tablespoon extra-virgin olive oil

2 garlic cloves, minced

½ teaspoon Chinese five-spice powder

2 tablespoons rice vinegar

½ teaspoon kosher salt

½ teaspoon red pepper flakes

1 tablespoon packed light brown sugar

1 tablespoon balsamic vinegar

1 teaspoon fresh ginger, peeled and chopped

¼ teaspoon white pepper

1 teaspoon sesame seeds

TO MAKE THE MARINADE

1. In a medium bowl, combine the molasses, soy sauce, olive oil, garlic, five-spice powder, rice vinegar, salt, red pepper flakes, brown sugar, balsamic vinegar, ginger, white pepper, and sesame seeds.

TO MAKE THE SHORT RIBS

2. Put the ribs in a gallon-size resealable plastic bag and pour in the marinade. Move the liquid around until the ribs are evenly covered. Refrigerate for up to 4 hours.

3. Prepare the smoker and preheat until the internal temperature reaches 225°F.

4. Once marinated, create a foil pouch by tearing off a piece of 18-by-18-inch heavy-duty foil.

5. Put the ribs in the center of the foil, on top of the shiny side. Fold the 4 sides on top of one another so that the ribs are loosely covered.

6. Insert a digital thermometer, then loosely seal the foil and put it directly on the smoker racks.

3 to 4 pounds beef short ribs

½ cup Cherry Barbecue Sauce (page 149)

7. Smoke for 4 to 5 hours, until the internal temperature reaches 205°F.

8. Remove the ribs from the smoker and let rest for 5 minutes before slicing and serving. Top with the barbecue sauce.

Sweet and Spicy Cheese-Stuffed Smoked Meatloaf

SERVES: **5 TO 6** / PREP TIME: **30 MINUTES** / SMOKE TIME: **3 TO 4 HOURS** / RECOMMENDED WOOD: **APPLE OR CHERRY**

Who would have thought you could smoke a meatloaf? Stuffed with both Cheddar and mozzarella cheeses, this meatloaf is easier to make than you might think. The key to rolling the stuffed meatloaf without making a mess is using parchment paper to guide you in the process. This recipe has a bit of a kick to it so I brush on a layer of my Kansas City–Style barbecue sauce to tame the heat. If you have any leftovers, make yourself a meatloaf sandwich topped with Garlic Aioli (page 159).

1 tablespoon extra-virgin olive oil

2 small onions, diced

4 garlic cloves, chopped

¾ cup panko bread crumbs

¾ cup 2% milk

2 large eggs, beaten

½ cup Kansas City–Style Barbecue Sauce (page 150), divided

2 tablespoons Worcestershire sauce

1 pound ground beef

1 pound ground pork

⅓ cup packed dark brown sugar

2 tablespoons smoked paprika

1 tablespoon onion powder

1 tablespoon garlic powder

1. In a medium skillet, heat the olive oil over medium-high heat for 2 to 3 minutes. Sauté the onions for 5 minutes. Add the garlic and sauté for another minute. Set the vegetables aside to cool.

2. In a large mixing bowl, combine the bread crumbs and milk so the bread crumbs absorb the liquid.

3. Add the eggs, ¼ cup of barbecue sauce, the Worcestershire sauce, ground beef, ground pork, brown sugar, paprika, onion powder, garlic powder, oregano, salt, pepper, chili powder, cumin, and cayenne pepper to the mixing bowl.

4. Mix gently with your hands until just combined.

5. Put the meatloaf mixture onto a piece of parchment paper and form a large, flat rectangle that is a quarter-inch thick.

6. Sprinkle both the Cheddar and mozzarella cheeses over the flattened meatloaf. Be sure to cover it edge to edge.

1 tablespoon dried oregano

1 tablespoon kosher salt

1 tablespoon black pepper

1 tablespoon chili powder

2 teaspoons ground cumin

½ teaspoon cayenne pepper

1 cup shredded Cheddar cheese

1 cup shredded mozzarella cheese

7. Starting from one edge of the parchment paper, carefully roll the meatloaf. As you roll it, peel back the parchment paper and continue rolling until you reach the end.

8. Transfer the meatloaf from the parchment paper to a grill pan. The grill pan should have holes or slits in the bottom so the smoke can pass through the bottom to the meat.

9. Prepare the smoker and preheat until the internal temperature reaches 225°F.

10. Put the meatloaf on the grill pan into the smoker and smoke for 3 to 4 hours, or until the internal temperature reaches 155°F.

11. Brush the remaining ¼ cup of barbecue sauce on the meatloaf and continue smoking for another 20 to 30 minutes until the sauce caramelizes and the internal temperature reaches 165°F.

12. Let rest for 5 minutes before slicing and serving.

EASY PREP TIP: When mixing, don't overwork the meat mixture—this will make your meatloaf dry out. Additionally, if you don't have a grill pan with holes, you can use a perforated pizza pan in a pinch.

STORAGE: Store covered in the refrigerator for up to 4 days. To serve, reheat the meatloaf in a 350°F oven for 15 minutes or until heated through.

Smoked Brisket

SERVES: 8 TO 10 / **PREP TIME:** 15 MINUTES (PLUS UP TO 4 HOURS TO MARINATE) /
SMOKE TIME: 8 TO 9 HOURS / **RECOMMENDED WOOD:** APPLE OR CHERRY

Brisket can seem intimidating, but it's actually not difficult to smoke at home. A simple dry rub and a bit of patience and you'll have yourself one succulent piece of meat. We're talking everyone's favorite smoked brisket recipe—that's how delicious this is. Brisket requires a longer smoke time and with that, you're probably going to experience the stall (see page 31 for a FAQ on stalling). But don't worry. I'm going to teach you how to get past that with a little secret.

1 (8- to 9-pound) brisket

½ cup Brisket Rub (page 153)

1. Put the brisket in a large glass dish or aluminum pan.

2. Generously apply the dry rub to the brisket, pressing firmly into the meat.

3. Cover the dish with either foil or plastic wrap and let marinate in refrigerator for at least 4 hours.

4. Prepare the smoker and preheat until the internal temperature reaches 225°F.

5. Put the brisket directly on the smoker racks, fat-side down, and insert a digital thermometer.

6. About 5 to 6 hours into the smoke, you may experience a stall in temperature. When this happens, pull the brisket out of the smoker and double wrap it with heavy-duty foil as tightly as possible. This will help maintain the internal heat and get past the stall.

7. Insert the meat thermometer back into the brisket and continue to smoke until the meat reaches 180°F.

8. Then, remove the brisket from the smoker and leave it wrapped in the foil. Wrap it in a towel over top of the foil. Put the wrapped brisket in an empty cooler to rest for 1 to 2 hours. This process helps make the brisket extra juicy and more tender.

9. After 2 hours, slice and serve.

EASY SMOKING TIP: You can estimate a smoke time of 1 hour per pound of brisket.

IF USING A GAS OR CHARCOAL SMOKER: Don't be surprised if you are not able to obtain a great smoke ring on a brisket when using an electric or pellet smoker. Smoke rings are produced by a chemical reaction between the pigment in the meat and the gases produced from the wood or charcoal.

Check the wood pan every 4 to 5 hours and add more chunks when needed. For this recipe I soak the wood chunks overnight, wrap them in heavy-duty foil before placing in the wood pan, and poke holes in the foil to allow the smoke to escape. I typically only have to add to my wood pan once with this recipe.

Mix 3 tablespoons of liquid smoke with 8 to 10 cups of water and pour into the smoker water pan. If using a pellet smoker, mix in 3 tablespoons of liquid smoke with 8 to 10 cups of water, pour into a disposable aluminum pan, and put it beside the meat directly on the smoker racks.

Smoked Brisket Burnt Ends with Cherry Barbecue Sauce

**SERVES: 4 TO 5 / PREP TIME: 30 MINUTES / SMOKE TIME: 4 TO 5 HOURS /
RECOMMENDED WOOD: APPLE, CHERRY, OR HICKORY**

Brisket has a reputation of being difficult to smoke. If you're wary about smoking a full brisket, why not start smaller and make brisket burnt ends? They're easy to smoke and only require a few steps. And talk about flavor—I once took a batch of these bite-size brisket burnt ends to a friend's house and after one bite he said, "I love the cherry flavor in the barbecue sauce, it's not too powerful. And the black pepper flavor in this one is spot-on." And he was right! The flavors are so distinguishable with every bite. My friend was popping these burnt ends in his mouth like they were candy—they are that good! You'll need a grilling basket for this recipe.

Extra-virgin olive oil,
for basting

1 (6-pound) brisket

½ cup Brisket Rub
(page 153), divided

1 cup Cherry Barbecue
Sauce (page 149), divided

2 tablespoons
salted butter

1. Baste the brisket with the olive oil.

2. Cover the brisket completely with ¼ cup of brisket rub.

3. With a sharp knife, cut the raw brisket into ¼-inch cubes.

4. Toss the cubes in the remaining ¼ cup of rub to ensure all sides are coated.

5. Put the brisket cubes in a barbecue grilling basket.

6. Prepare the smoker and preheat until the internal temperature reaches 250°F.

7. Put the basket in the smoker and insert a digital thermometer into a piece of brisket.

8. When the internal temperature of the brisket reaches 120°F, remove the grilling basket from the smoker.

9. Line a disposable aluminum pan with an extra-long piece of heavy-duty foil (long enough to fully wrap around the pan).

10. Remove the brisket pieces from the grilling basket and put them in the foil-lined pan.

11. Pour in ½ cup of barbecue sauce and brush the brisket pieces evenly.

12. Insert a digital thermometer into a piece of brisket, then fold the rest of the foil over the aluminum pan so the brisket is covered.

13. When it reaches 170°F, remove the pan from the smoker.

14. Remove the foil, leaving the burnt ends in the pan.

15. Add the butter and the remaining ½ cup of barbecue sauce to the brisket burnt ends.

16. Increase the smoker heat until it reaches 350°F. Stir and put the pan back into the smoker for 5 to 10 more minutes so that the burnt ends can crisp up.

17. Remove from the smoker and let rest for 10 minutes before serving. Brush on additional barbecue sauce, if desired.

STORAGE: Store covered in the refrigerator for up to 4 days. To serve, reheat in a 350°F oven for 20 minutes or until heated through.

Smoked Chuck Roast

**SERVES: 4 TO 5 / PREP TIME: 10 MINUTES / SMOKE TIME: 6 TO 8 HOURS /
RECOMMENDED WOOD: HICKORY OR PECAN**

While my sister and I were growing up, our mom always cooked a chuck roast in the oven on low heat for a roast beef Sunday dinner. But when I smoked a chuck roast for the first time, I was blown away at the taste difference. If you've never smoked a chuck roast, this is the recipe to try. During the smoking process, it forms the most succulent crust that is full of so much flavor it leaves you wanting more.

1 (5-pound) beef chuck roast

3 tablespoons extra-virgin olive oil

2 tablespoons House Seasoning (page 154)

1. Brush the olive oil on the chuck roast.

2. Completely cover the chuck roast with the house seasoning.

3. Prepare the smoker and preheat until the internal temperature reaches 225°F.

4. Put the roast directly onto the smoker racks and insert a digital thermometer.

5. Smoke the roast until the internal temperature reaches 200°F.

6. Remove the roast from the smoker and let rest for 10 minutes before slicing and serving.

EASY LEFTOVER TIP: This roast beef is amazing the next day served in a rice bowl with steamed broccoli topped with soy sauce. It's also great on a sandwich!

STORAGE: Store covered in the refrigerator for up to 4 days. To serve, reheat in a 350°F oven for 20 minutes or until heated through.

CHAPTER 4

POULTRY

Smoked Buffalo Chicken Wings 93

Sweet and Tangy Barbecue Smoked Chicken Wings 94

Smoked Chicken Drumsticks 96

Carolina Mustard Smoked Chicken Thighs 97

Hickory Smoked Barbecue Chicken Breasts 98

Applewood Smoked Chicken 100

Herbed Smoked Chicken Quarters 102

Honey-Orange Smoked Cornish Hen 103

Smoked Turkey Breast with Butter Herb Glaze 105

Cajun Smoked Whole Chicken 107

Roasted Herb Smoked Whole Turkey 110

Cherry Barbecue Smoked Duck 112

Parmesan Couscous–Stuffed Smoked Quail 114

When people think about smoking poultry, they often think of smoking a whole chicken or half chicken. But individual cuts of poultry are even easier to smoke, and they taste delicious. Chicken is a regular in my house—it's my go-to meat, and I serve it for dinner at least three times a week. It's lean, inexpensive, and can be flavored and cooked many different ways. And it's great for leftovers! Whether you're making drumsticks, thighs, breast, quarters, wings, or the entire chicken, it's all juicy and delicious when smoked.

This collection of smoked poultry recipes also includes meats like quail, turkey, and duck. A true variety, not only are these meats flavorful, but they are also easy enough for anyone to smoke, regardless of smoking experience. Using only simple ingredients, these are my tried-and-true poultry recipes that will have you coming back for seconds!

KEY POINTS TO REFERENCE WHEN SMOKING POULTRY

THAWED VERSUS FROZEN. Make sure the chicken is completely thawed before starting the smoking process. The texture and taste of the chicken will be off if the chicken isn't completely thawed before smoking.

POULTRY BREASTS AND THIGH TEMPERATURE. A lot of people overcook their chicken because they are scared of getting salmonella. All poultry (including the thighs and legs) is considered done when it reaches an internal temperature of 165°F. There's a lot of science and opinions around when chicken is truly done, but for the purpose of this book, my recommendation is to pull the chicken off the smoker when it reaches 165°F. Even one degree over can start to dry out the meat.

CHECKING FOR DONENESS. Always insert the digital thermometer into the thickest part of the meat you're smoking to get an accurate temperature reading. When the internal temperature of the chicken reaches 165°F, it's done.

TURNING CHICKEN. Depending on the size of the chicken pieces you're smoking, you may decide to flip and rotate the chicken periodically. I generally don't flip the chicken while it's smoking because I don't want to run the risk of the internal juices escaping due to movement, but I do flip chicken wings to get a crispy texture.

TRUSSING. We've all seen whole turkeys and chickens tied with twine around the drumsticks. This practice is called trussing. Trussing is mostly unnecessary for smoking purposes because tying the legs blocks the cavity of the bird and prevents air from circulating freely around the densest parts. However, if you are stuffing a whole chicken or turkey, trussing does help keep the stuffing from escaping during the smoking process.

SMOKING WHOLE VERSUS SPATCHCOCK. Spatchcocking is a method of cutting the chicken to remove the backbone so that it's opened up and can lay flat. Some advise that spatchcocking a chicken reduces the cooking time and helps cook the bird more evenly. There are recipes in this book to spatchcock a chicken as well as smoke a whole chicken so that you can try both methods.

Smoked Buffalo Chicken Wings

SERVES: 4 TO 6 / PREP TIME: 15 MINUTES / SMOKE TIME: 1 TO 2 HOURS / RECOMMENDED WOOD: APPLE OR CHERRY

If you like buffalo-style spicy chicken wings, then this is the recipe for you! These wings have a similar texture to the ones you find at restaurants, but they taste even better. Finish off the process by turning up the heat on your smoker. This method crisps up the skin while leaving the meat tender and juicy. You can use any sauce to accompany them, but they're perfect dipped in ranch or blue cheese dressing.

2 tablespoons chili powder

2 tablespoons smoked paprika

1 teaspoon ground cumin

1 teaspoon mustard powder

1 teaspoon onion powder

1 teaspoon garlic powder

2 teaspoons kosher salt

1 teaspoon freshly ground black pepper

2 tablespoons extra-virgin olive oil

12 to 15 appetizer-size chicken wings and drumsticks (1½ to 2 pounds total)

½ cup Frank's RedHot Original Cayenne Pepper Sauce, divided

1. In a small bowl, combine the chili powder, paprika, cumin, mustard powder, onion powder, garlic powder, salt, and pepper, then set aside.

2. With a basting brush, completely cover the wings and drumsticks with the olive oil.

3. Next, brush ¼ cup of the cayenne pepper sauce on each wing and drumstick, covering all sides.

4. Generously sprinkle the dry rub onto each wing and drumstick.

5. Prepare the smoker and preheat until the internal temperature reaches 225°F.

6. Put the wings and drumsticks directly on the smoker racks and insert a digital thermometer.

7. After 30 minutes, baste the wings and drumsticks with the remaining ¼ cup of cayenne pepper sauce.

8. When the internal temperature of the chicken reaches 155°F, turn the smoker up to an internal temperature of 350°F.

9. When the internal temperature of the chicken reaches 165°F, remove the wings from the smoker and let rest for 3 minutes before serving.

Sweet and Tangy Barbecue Smoked Chicken Wings

SERVES: 4 TO 6 / **PREP TIME:** 15 MINUTES / **SMOKE TIME:** 1 TO 2 HOURS / **RECOMMENDED WOOD:** APPLE OR CHERRY

These smoked chicken wings are filled with layers of flavor in every bite! You'll start out by smoking on a low temperature, but right before the wings are done, you'll need to turn up the heat so that the skin achieves a crisp texture.

2 tablespoons packed light brown sugar

1 teaspoon chili powder

1 teaspoon smoked paprika

½ teaspoon ground cumin

½ teaspoon onion powder

½ teaspoon garlic powder

½ teaspoon kosher salt

½ teaspoon freshly ground black pepper

12 to 15 appetizer-size chicken wings and drumsticks (1½ to 2 pounds total)

2 cups Kansas City–Style Barbecue Sauce (page 150)

1. In a small bowl, combine the brown sugar, chili powder, paprika, cumin, onion powder, garlic powder, salt, and pepper to make the dry rub.

2. Apply the dry rub to each wing and drumstick.

3. With a basting brush, slather each wing and drumstick with the barbecue sauce until completely covered.

4. Prepare the smoker and preheat until the internal temperature reaches 225°F.

5. Put the wings and drumsticks directly on the smoker racks and insert a digital thermometer.

6. Every 30 minutes, baste each side of the wings and drumsticks with the barbecue sauce.

7. When the internal temperature reaches 155°F, turn the temperature up until the internal heat of the smoker reaches between 350 and 400°F.

8. When the internal temperature of the chicken wings reaches 165°F, use a pair of tongs to remove them from the smoker and let rest for 3 minutes before serving.

EASY SMOKING TIP: If you want super-crispy smoked chicken wings, skip the barbecue sauce and other ingredients and just use 2 tablespoons of baking powder, 1 teaspoon of salt, and ½ teaspoon of freshly ground black pepper. Put the wings in a gallon-size resealable plastic bag and sprinkle in the dry ingredients. Shake well until the wings are evenly coated. Put the wings on the smoker and smoke at 250°F for 20 minutes. Increase the smoker temperature to 450°F and continue to smoke the wings for 35 to 40 more minutes, or until the chicken reaches an internal temperature of 165°F. Remove the wings from the smoker and let rest for 3 to 5 minutes. Serve alone or with your favorite barbecue sauce.

Smoked Chicken Drumsticks

SERVES: 5 TO 6 / **PREP TIME:** 10 MINUTES / **SMOKE TIME:** 2 TO 3 HOURS /
RECOMMENDED WOOD: APPLE OR CHERRY

If you're looking for a budget-friendly family meal, these chicken drumsticks are a great option. Not only are they inexpensive, but they're easy to find in any grocery store and go well with so many side dishes! Made with simple pantry ingredients, these drumsticks are perfect to take to any barbeque to share with family and friends.

8 chicken drumsticks

½ cup extra-virgin olive oil

1 teaspoon kosher salt

1 tablespoon dried oregano

1 tablespoon freshly ground black pepper

1½ teaspoons ground coriander

1 teaspoon smoked paprika

½ teaspoon ground cumin

1 teaspoon garlic powder

1. With a basting brush, completely cover the drumsticks with the olive oil and set aside.

2. In a small bowl, combine the salt, oregano, pepper, coriander, paprika, cumin, and garlic powder for the dry rub.

3. Apply the dry rub to each drumstick so that they are fully coated.

4. Prepare the smoker and preheat until the internal temperature reaches 225°F.

5. Put the drumsticks directly on the smoker racks and insert a digital thermometer.

6. When the internal temperature reaches 165°F, remove the chicken from the smoker and let rest for 3 minutes before serving.

STORAGE: Drumsticks freeze and reheat very well. Put any leftover chicken in a freezer-safe resealable plastic bag and store in the freezer for 3 to 4 months. To reheat, thaw them in the refrigerator, then reheat them in the oven at 350°F for 25 to 30 minutes or until they reach an internal temperature of 165°F.

Carolina Mustard Smoked Chicken Thighs

SERVES: 6 / PREP TIME: 10 MINUTES / SMOKE TIME: 2 TO 3 HOURS /
RECOMMENDED WOOD: APPLE OR CHERRY

The best chicken thighs I've ever tasted came from the smoker. Smoking pieces of chicken takes less time than smoking a whole chicken, and it's a lot easier and more convenient. I prefer to smoke bone-in chicken thighs because they tend to stay juicier than their boneless counterparts. While you can use any of my homemade barbecue sauces with this recipe, I love how the Carolina Mustard Barbecue Sauce tastes with this particular rub. These chicken thighs are perfect for any weeknight dinner or barbecue.

½ cup packed light brown sugar

1 teaspoon paprika

2 teaspoons smoked paprika

1 teaspoon freshly ground black pepper

1 tablespoon kosher salt

1 teaspoon garlic powder

1 teaspoon onion powder

1 teaspoon dry mustard

1 teaspoon dried marjoram

⅛ teaspoon cayenne pepper

6 (3- to 4-ounce) bone-in, skin-on chicken thighs

1 cup Carolina Mustard Barbecue Sauce (page 151)

1. In a small bowl, combine the brown sugar, paprika, smoked paprika, black pepper, salt, garlic powder, onion powder, dry mustard, marjoram, and cayenne pepper to make the dry rub.

2. Generously apply the dry rub onto the chicken until completely covered, ensuring to get the rub onto both sides and into all crevices.

3. Prepare the smoker and preheat until the internal temperature reaches 225°F.

4. Put the chicken directly on the smoker racks and insert a digital thermometer.

5. Every 30 minutes, baste the chicken thighs with the barbecue sauce.

6. When the internal temperature reaches 165°F, remove the chicken from the smoker and let rest for 3 minutes before serving.

EASY SERVING TIP: Smoked chicken thighs are also great shredded and can be used in sandwiches, casseroles, soups, and more. Using 2 forks, pull the cooked chicken into shreds. Remove any excess fat and discard the bones.

Hickory Smoked Barbecue Chicken Breasts

SERVES: 6 TO 8 / **PREP TIME:** 10 MINUTES (PLUS UP TO 1 HOUR TO BRINE) /
SMOKE TIME: 2 TO 3 HOURS / **RECOMMENDED WOOD:** APPLE

I make chicken breasts several times a week. They are so versatile, and the seasoning options are endless. When smoked on a low temperature, the tissue in the chicken breaks down, resulting in a very juicy piece of meat that melts in your mouth with every bite. And when you use a brine, it not only increases the tenderness but the meat actually absorbs all the flavors of the brining liquid. We're talking amazingly tender and tasty chicken!

Seasoned with a flavorful dry rub and smoked to a tender and juicy perfection, these chicken breasts are a family favorite with both adults and kids. I often pair this recipe with a side of my Smoked Baked Beans with Bacon (page 138) and Smoked Macaroni and Cheese (page 142)!

8 cups cold water

½ cup kosher salt

½ cup sugar

Juice of 1 lemon

6 to 8 (6- to 8-ounce) boneless, skinless chicken breasts

2 tablespoons garlic powder

1 teaspoon mustard powder

2 tablespoons smoked paprika

½ teaspoons freshly ground black pepper

½ teaspoon kosher salt

1 cup St. Louis–Style Barbecue Sauce (page 148)

1. In a large bowl, combine the water, salt, sugar, and lemon juice to create a brine.

2. Put the chicken breasts in a gallon-size resealable plastic bag, then pour in the brine and refrigerate for 1 hour.

3. After the brine time, remove the chicken and put it on paper towels to absorb the moisture.

4. In a small bowl, combine the garlic powder, mustard powder, paprika, pepper, and salt.

5. Apply the dry rub to each chicken breast, ensuring that both sides are completely covered.

6. Prepare the smoker and preheat until the internal temperature reaches 250°F.

7. Put the chicken breasts directly on the smoker racks and insert a digital thermometer.

8. After 45 minutes into the smoke, use a basting brush to slather the barbecue sauce on both sides of each chicken breast.

9. When the internal temperature reaches 165°F, remove the chicken from the smoker and let rest for 3 minutes before serving with additional barbecue sauce as desired.

EASY SERVING TIP: If you're feeding a lot of people, slice the chicken breasts into strips. This helps the chicken go a long way when you have a lot of guests!

Applewood Smoked Chicken

SERVES: 4 TO 5 / **PREP TIME:** 20 MINUTES (PLUS UP TO 2 HOURS TO MARINATE) /
SMOKE TIME: 4 TO 5 HOURS / **RECOMMENDED WOOD:** APPLE OR CHERRY

Who would have thought smoking an entire chicken could be so easy? You can either smoke it whole or spatchcock the chicken. Either way, it'll be juicy and delicious. Prepped with a brown sugar and smoked paprika rub, this Applewood Smoked Chicken tastes better than amazing! Easy, quick to prep, and incredibly tender, this smoked chicken is my most popular and most requested recipe.

¼ cup packed dark brown sugar

2 tablespoons chili powder

1 tablespoon smoked paprika

1 tablespoon onion powder

1 tablespoon garlic powder

1 tablespoon dried oregano

1 teaspoon kosher salt

1 (4- to 5-pound) whole chicken, thawed

1. In a small bowl, combine the brown sugar, chili powder, paprika, onion powder, garlic powder, oregano, and salt. Set aside.

2. Remove the internal parts (neck, liver, etc.) that are stuffed inside the chicken and discard them (or, you can reserve them to make a gravy).

3. Put the whole chicken on a cutting board, breast-side down.

4. To spatchcock the chicken, cut along the right of the backbone, then along the left side. Remove the backbone completely. Next, turn the chicken over, break the breastbone, and flatten the bird.

5. Put the spatchcocked chicken in a large glass dish or aluminum pan.

6. Generously apply the dry rub onto the chicken until completely covered, ensuring to get the rub onto both sides and into all crevices.

7. Cover the pan with plastic wrap and refrigerate for up to 4 hours.

8. Prepare the smoker and preheat until the internal temperature reaches 225°F.

9. Put the chicken directly on the smoker racks, breast-side up, and insert a digital thermometer.

10. When the internal temperature reaches 165°F, remove the chicken from the smoker and let rest for 3 to 5 minutes before slicing and serving.

EASY PREP TIP: It's not necessary to rinse a whole raw chicken and actually isn't good to do so because when water splashes, it can easily spread bacteria from the chicken into the sink and onto countertops.

STORAGE: Any leftover chicken can be covered and stored in the refrigerator for up to 4 days. To serve, reheat it in a 350°F oven for 20 minutes or until heated through.

Herbed Smoked Chicken Quarters

SERVES: 4 TO 6 / **PREP TIME:** 15 MINUTES / **SMOKE TIME:** 3 TO 4 HOURS /
RECOMMENDED WOOD: APPLE OR CHERRY

When it comes to grilling and smoking meat, chicken quarters are often neglected, which is a mystery to me because they are full of flavor and very juicy when smoked. There are 4 quarters of a chicken, but with this recipe I'm using the lower quarter consisting of the thigh and drumstick. Chicken quarters are inexpensive and sold bone-in with the skin still attached, and they're sold at most grocery stores.

¾ cup extra-virgin olive oil

2 teaspoons chopped
fresh thyme

2 teaspoon chopped fresh
rosemary

1 teaspoon whole
fennel seeds

2 teaspoons kosher salt

1 teaspoon freshly ground
black pepper

4 garlic cloves, minced

Juice of 1 lemon

4 chicken quarters, thigh
and drumstick
(1¼ pounds total)

1. In a small bowl, combine the olive oil, thyme, rosemary, fennel seeds, salt, pepper, garlic, and lemon juice for the wet rub.

2. Brush the wet rub on each chicken quarter completely. Set aside any leftover rub for basting.

3. Prepare the smoker and preheat until the internal temperature reaches 225°F.

4. Put the chicken directly on the smoker racks and insert a digital thermometer.

5. Twice during the smoke, baste each chicken quarter with the remaining wet rub.

6. When the internal temperature reaches 165°F, remove the chicken quarters from the smoker and let rest for 3 minutes before serving.

EASY PREP TIP: Since you're handling the chicken quarters a lot with this recipe, the last thing you want to do is grab a spice jar or bottle of olive oil with all that raw chicken on your hands. When making this recipe, I always premeasure the ingredients into individual bowls or ramekins so I don't have to worry about cross-contamination.

Honey-Orange Smoked Cornish Hen

**SERVES: 4 / PREP TIME: 15 MINUTES / SMOKE TIME: 1 TO 2 HOURS /
RECOMMENDED WOOD: APPLE OR PECAN**

The first time I ate smoked Cornish hen, I devoured it in no time flat. Shortly after, I decided to smoke my own. And oh my goodness, smoked Cornish hen has become one of my favorite meats to smoke. The honey-orange flavors in the wet rub are perfect for the hen and don't overpower the taste of the meat.

4 tablespoons (½ stick) salted butter, at room temperature

4 tablespoons packed light brown sugar

4 tablespoons honey

2 teaspoons smoked paprika

1 teaspoon kosher salt

½ teaspoon freshly ground black pepper

Juice of 1 orange

2 (1¼-pound) Cornish hens

1. In a small bowl, combine the butter, brown sugar, honey, paprika, salt, pepper, and orange juice to make the wet rub.

2. With a basting brush, brush each Cornish hen with the wet rub, ensuring you get in between all the crevices and cavities. Reserve the remaining wet rub for basting during smoking.

3. Prepare the smoker and preheat until the internal temperature reaches 225°F.

4. Put the chicken directly on the smoker racks and insert a digital thermometer.

5. Twice during the smoke, baste each Cornish hen with the wet rub.

6. When the internal temperature reaches 165°F, remove the Cornish hens from the smoker and let rest for 3 minutes before serving.

EASY SERVING TIP: While I can eat an entire Cornish hen on my own, I like to cut them in half so each person gets to enjoy half a hen. The easiest way to cut the hen is to put it on a large cutting board, then use a meat cleaver to cut it down the middle between the breasts. You'll want to apply a bit of pressure while using a slicing motion.

Smoked Turkey Breast with Butter Herb Glaze

SERVES: 4 TO 6 / **PREP TIME:** 10 MINUTES / **SMOKE TIME:** 3 TO 4 HOURS / **RECOMMENDED WOOD:** APPLE OR MAPLE

Smoking a turkey breast is one of the easiest ways to prepare turkey (and it's definitely a lot easier than smoking an entire bird). It's perfect for any meal and makes for the most amazing turkey sandwiches. Basted with a butter herb glaze, the turkey's flavor is over-the-top delicious!

¼ cup extra-virgin olive oil

4 garlic cloves, minced

2 teaspoons Himalayan salt, divided

2 tablespoons poultry seasoning

½ teaspoon freshly ground black pepper

1 (4- to 5-pound) boneless turkey breast

8 tablespoons (1 stick) unsalted butter, melted

2 tablespoons finely chopped fresh rosemary

1 tablespoon finely chopped fresh parsley

1 tablespoon finely chopped fresh thyme

1 tablespoon finely chopped fresh sage

1. In a small bowl, combine the olive oil, garlic, 1 teaspoon of salt, the poultry seasoning, and pepper to make the wet rub.

2. Baste the turkey breast completely with the wet rub.

3. In another small bowl, combine the butter, rosemary, parsley, thyme, sage, and the remaining 1 teaspoon of salt to make the brine. Set aside.

4. Prepare the smoker and preheat until the internal temperature reaches 225°F.

5. Put the turkey breast directly on the smoker racks and insert a digital thermometer.

6. Every hour during the smoke, baste the turkey breast with the brine.

CONTINUED ▶

7. When the internal temperature reaches 165°F, remove the turkey breasts from the smoker and let rest for 10 minutes before serving.

EASY SMOKING TIP: A lot of smoked meats have a pink hue once they have finished smoking due to the chemical changes that occur in the meat during the smoking process. As long as the internal temperature reaches 165°F at the thickest part of the meat, it's safe to eat.

STORAGE: Any leftover turkey can be covered and stored in the refrigerator for up to 4 days. To serve, reheat it in a 350°F oven for 20 minutes or until heated through.

Cajun Smoked Whole Chicken

SERVES: 4 TO 5 / **PREP TIME:** 20 MINUTES (PLUS UP TO 4 HOURS TO BRINE) /
SMOKE TIME: 4 TO 5 HOURS / **RECOMMENDED WOOD:** APPLE OR MAPLE

For this recipe, I prefer to smoke the whole chicken instead of spatchcocking it because it tastes like a rotisserie chicken—only better. The Cajun flavors are not overly spicy and are mild enough for any palette. I find that brining poultry, such as a whole turkey and chicken, adds additional aromatics and spices that you can taste in the meat. Brining with a hard cider or IPA brings out those flavors and also helps break down muscle proteins to make the meat more tender. And most important, it helps retain moisture during the slow smoking process.

FOR THE BRINE

4 cups water

1 pint apple cider beer

¼ cup packed dark brown sugar

4 garlic cloves, chopped

¼ cup kosher salt

1 tablespoon whole black peppercorns

1 (4- to 5-pound) whole chicken

FOR THE DRY RUB

2 tablespoons packed dark brown sugar

2 tablespoons smoked paprika

2 tablespoons kosher salt

1 tablespoon garlic powder

1 tablespoon dried oregano

1 teaspoon dried thyme

TO PREPARE THE BRINE

1. In a large bowl, combine the water, beer, brown sugar, garlic, salt, and peppercorns. Set aside.

2. Remove the internal parts (neck, liver, etc.) from inside the chicken and discard. If frozen, first thaw completely.

3. Put the whole chicken in the bowl with the brine and cover with plastic wrap.

4. Let it brine for at least 4 hours.

5. After the brine time, remove the chicken and put it in a large glass dish or aluminum pan.

TO PREPARE THE DRY RUB

6. In a small bowl, combine the brown sugar, paprika, salt, garlic powder, oregano, thyme, onion powder, black pepper, white pepper, and cayenne pepper. Mix well.

7. Generously apply the dry rub onto the chicken until it is completely covered, getting the rub onto both sides and into all crevices.

CONTINUED ▶

2 teaspoons onion powder

1 tablespoon freshly ground black pepper

1 teaspoon white pepper

½ teaspoon cayenne pepper

TO SMOKE THE CHICKEN

8. Prepare the smoker and preheat until the internal temperature reaches 250°F.

9. Put the whole chicken directly on the smoker racks, breast-side up, and insert a digital thermometer.

10. When the internal temperature reaches 165°F, remove the chicken from the smoker and let rest for 3 to 5 minutes before serving.

EASY SMOKING TIP: A lot of people love the taste of smoked chicken skin, but when smoked at a low temperature over a longer period of time, it often becomes rubbery. This Cajun-spiced skin is flavorful, so to get that skin crispy, turn the smoker temperature to high when the internal temperature of the chicken reaches 150°F. During the last few minutes on the smoker, the skin should get crispy without drying out the meat. Remove the chicken from the smoker when it reaches an internal temperature of 165°F.

STORAGE: Any leftover chicken can be covered and stored in the refrigerator for up to 4 days. To serve, reheat the chicken in a 350°F oven for 20 minutes or until heated through.

Roasted Herb Smoked Whole Turkey

**SERVES: 10 TO 12 / PREP TIME: 30 MINUTES / SMOKE TIME: 6 TO 7 HOURS /
RECOMMENDED WOOD: APPLE OR CHERRY**

The star of the show at Thanksgiving dinner, a whole turkey is anticipated by many for months in advance. And if it is smoked correctly, you'll never experience another dry turkey again. For this recipe, you'll need a flavor syringe so you can inject the marinade. You'll also apply softened butter to the turkey so the dry rub sticks. We're talking amazing flavor! As for the ingredients used to stuff the turkey, those enhance the flavor from the inside out. You can discard them once the turkey is finished smoking. When smoking a turkey, I always put a disposable aluminum pan under the turkey to catch the drippings, which are great for making a homemade turkey gravy!

FOR THE INJECTION MARINADE

8 tablespoons (1 stick) salted butter, at room temperature

⅓ cup extra-virgin olive oil

3 tablespoons Worcestershire sauce

½ cup water

3 tablespoons freshly squeezed lemon juice

1 teaspoon ground sage

½ teaspoon dried thyme

1 teaspoon garlic salt

1 teaspoon onion salt

TO MAKE THE INJECTION MARINADE

1. In a large bowl, combine the butter, olive oil, Worcestershire sauce, water, lemon juice, sage, thyme, garlic salt, and onion salt. Set aside.

TO MAKE THE DRY RUB

2. In a small bowl, combine the chili powder, paprika, garlic powder, onion salt, seasoning salt, and pepper. Set aside.

TO MAKE THE TURKEY

3. To prepare the turkey, remove the internal parts (neck, liver, etc.) and discard or save to make gravy.

4. Put the whole turkey in a large glass dish or aluminum pan.

5. Stuff the turkey with the rosemary, thyme, onion, and lemon.

2 tablespoons chili powder

2 tablespoons smoked paprika

2 tablespoons garlic powder

2 tablespoons onion salt

2 teaspoons seasoning salt

2 teaspoons freshly ground black pepper

FOR THE TURKEY

1 (12- to 15-pound) whole turkey

5 rosemary sprigs

3 thyme sprigs

1 onion, diced into quarters

1 lemon, halved

8 tablespoons (1 stick) unsalted butter, at room temperature

6. Fill a flavor syringe with the injection marinade and insert the syringe into the turkey breast 4 to 5 times in a line on each side of the breast, and twice on each leg. Do this until there is no marinade left.

7. Next, rub the butter all over the turkey.

8. Generously apply the dry rub onto the turkey until completely covered, ensuring the rub gets onto both sides and into all crevices.

9. Prepare the smoker and preheat until the internal temperature reaches 250°F.

10. Put the turkey on the smoker racks, breast-side up, and insert a digital thermometer.

11. When the internal temperature reaches 165°F, remove the turkey from the smoker and let rest for 7 to 10 minutes before serving.

EASY SMOKING TIP: It's so important to thaw the turkey properly and completely before you start the smoking process. If your turkey is frozen, put it in a large, deep aluminum pan in the refrigerator to thaw for 2 to 3 days before you start the smoking process. To ensure it's completely thawed, put your hands inside the bird to remove the neck and gizzard and have a good feel around inside. If the turkey feels soft and no longer frozen in places, the turkey is thawed. Plan on having the turkey smoke for about 30 minutes per pound.

Cherry Barbecue Smoked Duck

**SERVES: 2 TO 3 / PREP TIME: 30 MINUTES / SMOKE TIME: 2 TO 3 HOURS /
RECOMMENDED WOOD: CHERRY OR OAK**

Smoked duck is a delicacy everyone should experience. While it doesn't produce a lot of meat, the meat it does produce has a wonderful flavor. When paired with my Cherry Barbecue Sauce, it becomes an absolute taste revelation! I stuff the duck with fresh lemongrass, shallot, garlic, and lime wedges to produce flavors from the inside out. Smoked duck tastes amazing with a side of steamed rice and roasted vegetables, and it's perfect for the holidays or when celebrating a special occasion.

2 cups water

1 (5-pound) whole duck

1 stalk fresh lemongrass

1 shallot, chopped

1 lime, cut into wedges

3 garlic cloves, crushed

2 cups Cherry Barbecue Sauce (page 149), divided

1. Put a wire rack or barbecue grilling basket in a disposable aluminum pan. Fill the pan with the water and set aside.

2. Remove the neck from the duck and stuff the duck with the lemongrass, shallot, lime, and garlic.

3. Baste the duck with ½ cup of the barbecue sauce, basting onto both sides and into all crevices.

4. Put the duck on the barbecue grilling basket in the aluminum pan, breast-side up.

5. Prepare the smoker and preheat until the internal temperature reaches 300°F.

6. Put the aluminum pan on the smoker racks and insert a digital thermometer into the duck breast.

7. Every 30 minutes, baste the duck with the barbecue sauce.

8. When the internal temperature reaches 165°F, remove the duck from the smoker and let rest for 5 minutes before serving.

EASY SMOKING TIP: When smoking most meats, I tend to keep the smoker temperature low, but when smoking duck, I keep the smoker at 300°F. Duck has a higher level of fat, and when smoked at a slightly higher temperature, it helps liquify the fat and make the meat moist. Since the fat renders pretty easily with duck, I sometimes skip the barbecue sauce baste and use the drippings in the pan to make my own homemade gravy!

Parmesan Couscous–Stuffed Smoked Quail

**SERVES: 4 / PREP TIME: 45 MINUTES / SMOKE TIME: 45 MINUTES TO 1 HOUR /
RECOMMENDED WOOD: APPLE OR CHERRY**

I get excited about smoking quail because it's such a versatile piece of meat.
Quail are delicate little birds that are perfect for stuffing because the breast bone
has been removed. For this recipe, I stuff the quail with a Parmesan couscous and
coat each piece with a mixture of coriander and olive oil. You'll need twine to tie
the wings and legs to ensure the stuffing doesn't seep out while smoking. If
you've never smoked quail before, then this recipe is a must!

1 box Parmesan couscous

4 quail

¼ cup extra-virgin olive oil

**½ teaspoon ground
coriander**

**2 teaspoons
Himalayan salt**

1. Prepare the couscous according to package
   directions; set aside.

2. Put each quail in a glass dish or baking sheet.

3. Stuff each quail with 2 tablespoons of couscous.

4. With a piece of twine, tie the top of the legs
   together to close the opening at the bottom of
   the quail.

5. With another piece of twine, tie the top of the wings
   together to close the opening on the top of the
   quail. You want to ensure the stuffing does not come
   out during the smoke.

6. In a small bowl, combine the olive oil and coriander.

7. Using a basting brush, brush both sides of each
   quail with the olive oil mixture.

8. Prepare the smoker and preheat until the internal
   temperature reaches 225°F.

9. Put each quail directly on the smoker racks,
   breast-side up, and insert a digital thermometer into
   the leg of a quail.

10. When the internal temperature reaches 155°F, remove the quail from the smoker and let the quail rest for 3 minutes before serving.

EASY INGREDIENT TIP: If you're a big stuffing fan like I am, you can increase the amount of stuffing to ¼ cup of couscous; feel free to use any flavor of boxed couscous.

CHAPTER 5

FISH & SEAFOOD

Garlic Butter Smoked Shrimp 118

Blackened Smoked Catfish 119

Orange Honey-Glazed Smoked Salmon 121

Smoked Ahi Tuna 123

Bacon-Wrapped Smoked Scallops 124

Orange-Ginger Smoked Halibut 126

Smoked Coconut Shrimp 128

Smoked Lobster Tail 129

Smoked Mahi-Mahi Soft Tacos with Corn Salsa 131

Parmesan-Crusted Smoked Tilapia 133

Smoked Crab Legs 134

Smoking fish and seafood might seem intimidating, but it's actually not, especially if you're interested in trying seafood prepared a different way that isn't baked, sautéed, or grilled. But if you've never smoked fish or other types of seafood before, then you're in for a real treat with this chapter.

Smoking seafood is easy, generally takes under two hours, and is perfect any day of the week! Lobster tail, scallops, shrimp, salmon, and even ahi tuna—I've infused these recipes with loads of flavor, freshness, and variety that the entire family will enjoy! I'm going to introduce a lot of new brines and seasonings in this chapter that pair exceptionally well with a variety of seafood, and we'll finish off this chapter with a delicious vegetarian smoked side dish that pairs perfectly with any seafood recipe.

Garlic Butter Smoked Shrimp

**SERVES: 4 / PREP TIME: 10 MINUTES / SMOKE TIME: 30 TO 45 MINUTES /
RECOMMENDED WOOD: APPLE OR CHERRY**

The simplest ingredients give you absolutely the most flavorful and mouth-watering smoked shrimp! I use a simple garlic butter sauce to provide a light flavor and then put the shrimp in a disposable aluminum pan to smoke. In less than an hour, you'll have amazingly tasty shrimp for any meal. These shrimp are not only delicious eaten on their own, but I often add them to other dishes such as pasta, stir fry, or in tacos.

1 pound raw large shrimp, peeled and deveined, with tails attached

1 cup Seafood Garlic Butter Sauce (page 157)

1. Put the shrimp in a single layer in a disposable aluminum pan.

2. With a basting brush, apply the garlic butter sauce onto both sides of the shrimp, reserving some of the sauce for basting during smoking.

3. Prepare the smoker and preheat until the internal temperature reaches 225°F.

4. Put the pan with the shrimp directly on the smoker racks and smoke for 30 to 45 minutes, until a digital thermometer reads 120°F.

5. Twice during the smoke, baste the shrimp with the butter sauce.

6. Once done, remove the shrimp from the smoker and serve immediately.

EASY SMOKING TIP: For added moisture and more flavor, I add 6 tablespoons of melted butter to the bottom of the aluminum pan with a little bit of salt before placing the shrimp in the pan to smoke. I turn them once during the smoking process to ensure both sides are smoked in the buttery goodness! You can also squeeze fresh lime juice onto the shrimp during and after the smoking period to add a refreshing citrus flavor.

Blackened Smoked Catfish

SERVES: 4 TO 5 / PREP TIME: 15 MINUTES / SMOKE TIME: 1 TO 2 HOURS / RECOMMENDED WOOD: ALDER OR APPLE

Blackened is a method of coating meat in butter, then adding a variety of seasonings and spices before it's cooked. Food that has been blackened is very flavorful and can be a bit on the spicy side. This Blackened Smoked Catfish is a flaky and flavorful masterpiece. Don't skip the lemon—it adds a bit of acidity to help balance out the spiciness.

2 tablespoons unsalted butter, melted

Juice of ½ lemon

4 to 5 (5- to 7-ounce) catfish fillets

1½ teaspoons smoked paprika

1½ teaspoons garlic powder

1 teaspoon onion powder

½ tablespoon freshly ground black pepper

½ teaspoon dried thyme

½ teaspoon Italian seasoning

½ teaspoon dried oregano

⅛ teaspoon cayenne pepper

½ teaspoon kosher salt

1. In a small bowl, combine the melted butter and lemon juice.

2. With a basting brush, brush the lemon butter mixture onto each catfish fillet.

3. In a small bowl, combine the paprika, garlic powder, onion powder, black pepper, thyme, Italian seasoning, oregano, cayenne pepper, and salt to make a dry rub.

4. Sprinkle the rub to cover both sides of the fish. Set aside.

5. Prepare the smoker and preheat until the internal temperature reaches 225°F.

6. Put the fish directly on the smoker racks and insert a digital thermometer.

7. When the internal temperature reaches 145°F, remove the catfish from the smoker and serve immediately.

EASY SMOKING TIP: I find that catfish is easier to smoke with the skin removed. While you can smoke it directly on the smoker racks, I like to use a grilling basket, as the fish tends to be flaky.

Orange Honey-Glazed Smoked Salmon

SERVES: 4 / **PREP TIME:** 20 MINUTES (PLUS UP TO 2 HOURS TO BRINE AND REST) /
SMOKE TIME: 3 TO 4 HOURS / **RECOMMENDED WOOD:** APPLE OR MAPLE

Salmon is simple to smoke, and this version has an incredibly flaky texture with the most wonderful citrus flavor and a hint of sweetness. For this recipe, I brine the salmon in fresh orange and lemon juice so it can absorb the citrus flavors. During the smoke, I slather on the glaze to enhance the flavors even more!

When smoking salmon, I prefer the skin to be attached. Both Atlantic and sockeye salmon are excellent choices to use with this recipe. If you're using skinless salmon for this recipe, put it on a piece of heavy-duty foil before placing it in the smoker.

¾ cup honey, divided

Juice of 2 oranges, divided

1 tablespoon balsamic vinegar

1 tablespoon chopped fresh rosemary

¼ teaspoon freshly ground black pepper

¼ teaspoon Himalayan salt

6 cups cool water

¼ cup packed light brown sugar

4 tablespoons plus ¼ teaspoon sea salt, divided

Grated zest of ½ orange

Juice of ½ lemon

4 (6-ounce) salmon fillets

1. In a small bowl, combine ¼ cup of honey, the juice of 1 orange, the balsamic vinegar, rosemary, pepper, and Himalayan salt for the glaze. Set aside.

2. In a large bowl, combine the water, remaining ½ cup of honey, the brown sugar, 4 tablespoons of sea salt, the juice of the remaining the orange, the orange zest, and lemon juice to make the brine.

3. Put the brine and the salmon pieces in a gallon-size resealable plastic bag and let it brine for 1 hour.

4. Remove the salmon from the brine and transfer to a cooling rack positioned over a baking sheet. Cover the salmon with plastic wrap and put it in the refrigerator to rest for 2 hours.

5. After the rest period, season the salmon with the remaining ¼ teaspoon of sea salt.

CONTINUED ▶

6. Baste each salmon fillet with an even layer of the honey orange glaze, reserving some for basting during smoking.

7. Prepare the smoker and preheat until the internal temperature reaches 180°F.

8. Put the salmon directly on the smoker grates, skin-side down, and insert a digital thermometer.

9. Every hour during the smoke, baste the salmon with the glaze.

10. When the internal temperature reaches 145°F, remove the salmon from the smoker and serve immediately.

EASY INGREDIENT TIP: When you buy salmon from a supermarket, most of the bones will have been removed, but I always like to check to be sure. To check for bones, gently bend the raw fillet and run your fingers over the surface of the fillet; any bones will stick out from the skin and you can gently remove them with a pair of tweezers or your fingers.

Smoked Ahi Tuna

**SERVES: 4 / PREP TIME: 10 MINUTES (PLUS UP TO 1 HOUR TO BRINE) /
SMOKE TIME: 30 TO 45 MINUTES / RECOMMENDED WOOD: APPLE OR CHERRY**

While I like canned tuna on top of a salad or in a sandwich, I prefer fresh tuna for smoking. The USDA recommends consuming tuna when it reaches an internal temperature of 140 to 145°F, but I enjoy smoked ahi tuna at a medium-rare temperature (around 125°F). Brined in a light white wine sauce and then seasoned with the simplest ingredients, this smoked ahi tuna shines on top of a salad or in a sushi roll. I also enjoy using this tuna recipe mixed with mayonnaise for a delicious fresh tuna sandwich!

6 cups water

1 cup sauvignon blanc wine

3 tablespoons plus ¼ teaspoon kosher salt

¼ cup packed light brown sugar

Juice of 1 lemon

3 rosemary sprigs

4 (6-ounce) ahi tuna fillets

3 tablespoons extra-virgin olive oil

¼ teaspoon freshly ground black pepper

1. In a large bowl, combine the water, wine, 3 tablespoons of salt, the brown sugar, and lemon juice to make the brine.

2. Pour the brine into a gallon-size resealable plastic bag, then put the ahi tuna pieces in the bag for 1 hour.

3. Remove the tuna from the brine and put it on paper towels to absorb the excess liquid.

4. With a basting brush, apply the olive oil to all sides of the tuna and sprinkle on the pepper and the remaining ¼ teaspoon of salt.

5. Prepare the smoker and preheat until the internal temperature reaches 190°F.

6. Put the tuna fillets directly on the smoker racks and insert a digital thermometer.

7. When the internal temperature reaches 125°F, remove the fish from the smoker and serve immediately.

Bacon-Wrapped Smoked Scallops

**SERVES: 4 TO 5 / PREP TIME: 20 MINUTES / SMOKE TIME: 45 MINUTES TO 1 HOUR /
RECOMMENDED WOOD: APPLE OR CHERRY**

Scallops are elegant and sophisticated yet easy to make. They are perfect for special occasions as an appetizer or even as a fun weeknight meal. Wrapped in bacon and slathered with a simple garlic baste, these scallops smoke in about an hour and are amazing on top of risotto. When smoking scallops, it's important to ensure they stay moist. I always put a pan of water in the smoker so the scallops can absorb the extra moisture, which keeps them from becoming tough and chewy.

2 tablespoons extra-virgin olive oil

¼ teaspoon garlic powder

¼ teaspoon freshly ground black pepper

12 sea scallops

12 slices pork bacon

Chopped parsley, for garnish

1. In a small bowl, combine the olive oil, garlic powder, and pepper.

2. Put the scallops in a single layer in a disposable aluminum pan.

3. With a basting brush, apply the olive oil mixture onto all sides of each scallop.

4. Wrap a piece of bacon around each scallop and secure with a toothpick. Repeat this process for each scallop.

5. Prepare the smoker and preheat until the internal temperature reaches 210°F.

6. Put the pan on the smoker racks and insert a digital thermometer into one of the scallops.

7. When the internal temperature reaches 145°F, remove the scallops from the smoker. Garnish the scallops with the parsley and serve immediately.

EASY SMOKING TIP: If using a gas or charcoal smoker, add 6 to 8 cups of water to the smoker water pan. If using an electric or pellet smoker, pour the water into a disposable aluminum pan and put it beside the scallops directly on the smoker racks. This will ensure the scallops are kept extra-moist while smoking.

INGREDIENT TIP: If you prefer crispier bacon, pan sear the bacon in a cast-iron skillet before wrapping it around each scallop.

Orange-Ginger Smoked Halibut

SERVES: 4 / **PREP TIME:** 20 MINUTES (PLUS UP TO 2 HOURS TO BRINE) /
SMOKE TIME: 1 TO 2 HOURS / **RECOMMENDED WOOD:** ALDER OR OAK

Halibut is a large fish that yields large fillets. This white fish contains little fat, yet it is very flavorful on its own, which is why I keep the ingredients simple in this recipe. Purchasing halibut can be expensive, so I tend to make this Orange-Ginger Smoked Halibut on special occasions. Easy, quick, and delicious, this recipe tastes amazing served with simple side dishes such as rice and asparagus.

8 cups cold water

Juice of 2 oranges, divided

Juice of 2 limes

¼ cup packed light brown sugar

4 halibut fillets (about 2 pounds total)

1 teaspoon kosher salt

1 teaspoon ginger paste

2 tablespoons honey

1. In a large bowl, combine the cold water, juice of 1 orange, the lime juice, and brown sugar to make the brine.

2. Pour the brine into a gallon-size resealable plastic bag, then put the halibut in the bag and let it brine for 2 hours.

3. After brining is complete, remove the halibut and place it on a large dish.

4. In a medium bowl, combine the juice of the remaining orange, the salt, ginger paste, and honey. Reserve some of the mixture for basting during smoking.

5. Using a basting brush, apply the orange juice and ginger mixture to each side of the halibut fillets.

6. Prepare the smoker and preheat until the internal temperature reaches 200°F.

7. Put each fillet on a piece of heavy-duty foil.

8. Put the foil directly on the smoker racks and insert a digital thermometer into a piece of halibut.

9. When the internal temperature of the fish reaches 90°F, baste each halibut fillet with the orange juice and ginger baste. Repeat this process once more when the internal temperature reaches 120°F.

10. When the internal temperature reaches 140°F, remove the halibut from the smoker and serve immediately.

EASY SMOKING TIP: When smoking halibut, there is a narrow window between moist and flaky fish and dried-out fish. Pull the halibut off the smoker as soon as it reaches 140°F and not one degree over.

Smoked Coconut Shrimp

**SERVES: 4 TO 6 / PREP TIME: 30 MINUTES / SMOKE TIME: 45 MINUTES /
RECOMMENDED WOOD: APPLE**

This coconut shrimp recipe is great for an appetizer, lunch, or dinner! Dipped in coconut milk and then rolled in bread crumbs and sweetened shredded coconut, these shrimp are smoked to a golden perfection. While this recipe isn't overly sweet, you can easily add to the sweetness if you prefer by dipping the shrimp in honey after they've been smoked.

1 cup unsweetened full-fat coconut milk

1 cup sweetened shredded coconut

½ teaspoon sea salt

¼ teaspoon freshly ground black pepper

1 cup panko bread crumbs

1 pound raw large shrimp, peeled and deveined, with tails attached

1. Pour the coconut milk into a large bowl and the shredded coconut into a separate large bowl.

2. In another large bowl, combine the salt, pepper, and bread crumbs.

3. Submerge one shrimp in the coconut milk, then roll the shrimp in the breadcrumb mixture to coat evenly.

4. Put the shrimp in the shredded coconut and press firmly until the shrimp is lightly coated.

5. Put the shrimp on a baking sheet and repeat this process for each shrimp.

6. Prepare the smoker and preheat until the internal temperature reaches 225°F.

7. Put the baking sheet directly on the smoker racks.

8. Smoke the shrimp on a baking sheet for 30 to 45 minutes.

9. Once done, remove the baking sheet from the smoker and serve.

EASY PREP TIP: To add a bit more crunch, broil the shrimp in the oven on high heat after smoking until they turn a light golden brown.

Smoked Lobster Tail

**SERVES: 4 TO 5 / PREP TIME: 30 MINUTES / SMOKE TIME: 45 MINUTES TO 1 HOUR /
RECOMMENDED WOOD: APPLE OR CHERRY**

Smoked to tender perfection, this garlic butter lobster tail isn't only super simple to prepare but also easy to smoke. The key to getting juicy and tender lobster meat involves cutting the shell with a pair of kitchen shears. This allows the smoke to penetrate the meat while providing a way for you to baste with the butter sauce.

4 to 5 (6- to 7-ounce) lobster tails

¾ cup Seafood Garlic Butter Sauce (page 157)

Melted butter, for serving

Freshly squeezed lemon juice, for serving

1. With a pair of kitchen shears, cut the shell on top of the lobster to expose the meat. Use your finger to gently run alongside the inner part of the shell to detach the meat.

2. With a basting brush, apply the garlic butter sauce onto the lobster meat, reserving some of the sauce for basting during smoking.

3. Prepare the smoker and preheat until the internal temperature reaches 250°F.

4. Put each lobster tail directly on the smoker racks, meat-side up.

5. Twice during the smoke, baste each lobster with the garlic butter sauce.

6. When the internal temperature reaches 140°F, remove the lobster from the smoker and let rest for 5 minutes.

7. Then, slide a fork underneath the lobster meat to lift it up. Serve with melted butter and freshly squeezed lemon juice.

EASY SMOKING TIP: While it's best to clean your smoker after each smoke, lobster easily soaks up the flavor it's exposed to, so make sure you clean your smoker beforehand.

Smoked Mahi-Mahi Soft Tacos with Corn Salsa

SERVES: 4 TO 6 / PREP TIME: 30 MINUTES / SMOKE TIME: 30 TO 45 MINUTES / RECOMMENDED WOOD: APPLE OR CHERRY

Using mahi-mahi in fish tacos isn't only easy but also super tasty! I kept the seasoning simple with this recipe and used a prepared Cajun seasoning that you can find at your local grocery store. I like serving these smoked mahi-mahi tacos on soft corn tortillas topped with a simple corn salsa made with sweet peppers, avocado, and fresh corn. It only takes about 45 minutes to smoke mahi-mahi, which makes this recipe perfect for any weeknight dinner!

FOR THE CORN SALSA

2 cups corn, canned, fresh, or thawed

1 avocado, diced

½ red bell pepper, diced

½ green bell pepper, diced

1 tomato, diced

2 tablespoons diced red onion

¼ teaspoon ground cumin

¼ teaspoon smoked paprika

¼ teaspoon sea salt

¼ teaspoon freshly ground black pepper

2 tablespoons extra-virgin olive oil

2 teaspoons freshly squeezed lime juice

TO MAKE THE CORN SALSA

1. In a large bowl, combine the corn, avocado, bell peppers, tomato, onion, cumin, paprika, salt, pepper, olive oil, lime juice, and cilantro. Store covered in the refrigerator until the fish is finished smoking. Just before serving, crumble the cheese on top.

TO PREPARE THE FISH

2. Apply the Cajun seasoning on all sides of the fish. Squeeze 2 lemon wedges over the fish, then set aside.

3. Prepare the smoker and preheat until the internal temperature reaches 225°F.

4. Put each piece of fish directly on the smoker racks.

5. When the internal temperature reaches 145°F, remove the fish from the smoker.

CONTINUED ▶

1 tablespoon chopped fresh cilantro

1 to 2 tablespoons cotija cheese, crumbled

FOR THE FISH

4 (4- to 6-ounce) mahi-mahi fillets

2 tablespoons Cajun seasoning

3 lemon wedges, divided

Corn tortillas, for serving

6. Serve the mahi-mahi on a platter to make fish tacos, then top them with the fresh corn salsa.

7. Squeeze the remaining lemon wedge onto the corn salsa.

Parmesan-Crusted Smoked Tilapia

**SERVES: 4 / PREP TIME: 20 MINUTES / SMOKE TIME: 1 TO 2 HOURS /
RECOMMENDED WOOD: APPLE OR ALDER**

You typically see smoker recipes made with brines, marinades, and bastes. But coating a piece of meat seasoned with flavored bread crumbs is delicious and provides crunchiness in every bite! While tilapia has a semi-firm texture, it also has a mild, sweet flavor. It's an inexpensive fish that's quick to prep and perfect for any weeknight dinner.

¼ cup shredded
Parmesan cheese

1 teaspoon garlic powder

1 teaspoon smoked paprika

2 teaspoons kosher salt

1 teaspoon Italian
seasoning

1 teaspoon freshly ground
black pepper

2 cups panko bread crumbs

1 tablespoon dried parsley

4 (6-ounce) tilapia fillets

1. In a small bowl, combine the Parmesan cheese, garlic powder, paprika, salt, Italian seasoning, pepper, bread crumbs, and parsley to make the dry rub.

2. Apply the dry rub to cover both sides of the fish. Set aside.

3. Prepare the smoker and preheat until the internal temperature reaches 225°F.

4. Put the tilapia directly on the smoker racks and insert a digital thermometer.

5. When the internal temperature reaches 145°F, remove the fish from the smoker and serve immediately.

EASY SMOKING TIP: To get crispier bread crumbs, put the smoked tilapia in the oven and broil on high for 3 to 4 minutes after smoking, until the crust starts to turn a light golden brown.

Smoked Crab Legs

**SERVES: 4 / PREP TIME: 30 MINUTES / SMOKE TIME: 30 TO 45 MINUTES /
RECOMMENDED WOOD: APPLE OR CHERRY**

I prefer Alaskan king crab legs for this recipe because the texture of the meat is a bit more delicate and tender. I also find that it has a sweeter taste. For this recipe, you'll need a seafood cracker and a small fork so you can get the meat out of the knuckles and pincers. For the rest of the crab, it's just as easy to use your hands to crack the legs. Once the shells are cracked, the meat just pulls right out! Topped with a butter sauce and lemon juice, these crab legs are perfect to eat any day of the week.

4 pounds crab legs

1 cup Seafood Garlic Butter Sauce (page 157)

Melted butter, for serving

Lemon wedges, for serving

1. On a baking sheet, cut the king crab legs open about 2 inches.

2. With a basting brush, apply the garlic butter sauce to the crab legs, reserving some for basting during smoking.

3. Prepare the smoker and preheat until the internal temperature reaches 225°F.

4. Put each crab leg directly on the smoker racks, cut-side up.

5. Twice during the smoke, baste the king crab with the seafood butter sauce.

6. After 30 minutes, remove the crab legs from the smoker and let rest for 5 minutes.

7. Serve with melted butter and lemon wedges.

EASY INGREDIENT TIP: If you don't have a seafood cracker, you can use your hands to crack crab legs. Using both hands, snap the crab leg like you are trying to break it in half. Once you hear a cracking sound, wiggle the shell back and forth and then gently pull outward to remove the crab meat.

CHAPTER 6

SIDES, SAUCES, RUBS & MARINADES

Smoked Baked Beans with Bacon 138

Cracked Pepper Beef Jerky 139

Smoked Herbed Potatoes 141

Smoked Macaroni and Cheese 142

Smoked Cherry Tomatoes with Basil and Goat Cheese 143

Homestyle Barbecue Sauce 147

St. Louis–Style Barbecue Sauce 148

Cherry Barbecue Sauce 149

Kansas City–Style Barbecue Sauce 150

Carolina Mustard Barbecue Sauce 151

Tarragon Dijon Sauce 152

Brisket Rub 153

House Seasoning 154

Boston Butt Rub 155

Montreal Dry Rub 156

Seafood Garlic Butter Sauce 157

Tzatziki Sauce 158

Garlic Aioli 159

Give your smoked meat some extra flavor with these easy sauces, rubs, and marinades! Every recipe you'll find in this chapter is used in at least one, if not more, of the meat recipes throughout the book. When creating rubs and sauces, my philosophy is to use *simple* ingredients that are flavor-packed and easy to find at your local grocery store. You'll see that a lot of the recipes I include in this chapter contain the basics such as smoked paprika, garlic powder, and cumin to bring forth a lot of flavor. I also use fresh herbs such as chopped rosemary and thyme to pull out certain flavors that enhance the taste of smoked meat. When it comes to ingredients, if I can't clearly distinguish the flavor or if it doesn't enhance the overall taste of the meat, I don't include it.

As you'll see, it doesn't take complicated ingredients to make wonderful sauces, rubs, and marinades. It all starts with simple ingredients that are easy to find and recipes that are easy to make. Versatility is key. Each one of the recipes in this chapter can be applied to a variety of different smoked foods and can be used over and over again.

You can create a majority of these sauces and rubs in advance so that when you're ready to start smoking meat, you've already saved yourself time in the preparation process. When making dry rubs, store them in an airtight container until ready for use. Dry rubs will last up to six months if stored in a cool, dry place. When making barbecue sauces, I typically store them in glass mason jars and refrigerate until I'm ready to use them. Barbecue sauces can be stored in the refrigerator for up to three weeks after preparation.

Smoked Baked Beans with Bacon

SERVES: 10 TO 12 / PREP TIME: 20 MINUTES / SMOKE TIME: 2 HOURS /
RECOMMENDED WOOD: APPLE OR CHERRY

This is a Southern-style recipe that's been in my life since my college years. My best friend Holly's grandmother has been making these beans since the early 1980s. She makes hers in the oven, but I've adapted this classic into a delicious smoker recipe that's not only an easy side dish, but also big enough to feed a crowd and perfect for any barbecue!

1 (53-ounce) can of Van Camp's pork and beans (or any other brand)

¼ cup packed light brown sugar

¼ cup molasses

2 tablespoons yellow mustard

1 small onion, finely chopped

1 (16-ounce) package pork bacon

1. In a large bowl, combine the pork and beans, brown sugar, molasses, mustard, and onion.

2. Pour the mixture into a disposable aluminum pan.

3. Chop the bacon into 2-inch pieces and lay them on top of the baked bean mixture.

4. Prepare the smoker and preheat until the internal temperature reaches 225°F.

5. Put the uncovered aluminum pan in the smoker and smoke for 2 hours.

6. When done, the bacon should be golden brown around the edges.

7. Stir with a spoon to incorporate the smoked bacon and serve immediately.

STORAGE: Store leftovers covered in the refrigerator for 4 to 5 days. To serve, reheat in a 350°F oven for 20 minutes or until heated through.

Cracked Pepper Beef Jerky

SERVES: 8 TO 10 / PREP TIME: 30 MINUTES (PLUS UP TO 4 HOURS TO MARINATE) / SMOKE TIME: 3 TO 4 HOURS / RECOMMENDED WOOD: HICKORY

Learn how to make your own beef jerky at home in your own smoker! Marinated in dark IPA with several types of pepper, this beef jerky is tender, full of flavor, and irresistible. It's the perfect high-protein, low-carb snack.

2 pounds top round beef

1½ cups dark IPA beer

¼ cup soy sauce

2 tablespoons Worcestershire sauce

½ teaspoon garlic salt

2 tablespoons packed dark brown sugar

2 tablespoons freshly ground black pepper

1 teaspoon white pepper

1. Cut the beef across the grain into ¼-inch-thick slices and set aside. Or, have the butcher slice the meat.

2. In a medium bowl, combine the beer, soy sauce, Worcestershire sauce, garlic salt, brown sugar, black pepper, and white pepper.

3. Put the steak in a gallon-size resealable plastic bag and pour in the marinade. Move the liquid around until the steak is well covered.

4. Refrigerate and let it marinate for up to 4 hours.

5. After the steak has marinated, remove each piece of steak and put it on paper towels.

6. Prepare the smoker and preheat until the internal temperature reaches 180°F.

7. Put each piece of steak on the smoker racks and smoke for 3 to 4 hours.

8. One hour into smoking, check to ensure the jerky is drying appropriately. The jerky should begin to get firm, yet still slightly pliable.

9. After 3 to 4 hours, remove the jerky from the smoker.

CONTINUED ▸

10. Put the finished jerky in a gallon-size resealable plastic bag while still warm. Seal the baggie halfway so that a little air can enter while the jerky is still hot. This steam will help keep the jerky moist.

EASY COOKING TIP: It can be difficult to gauge the internal temperature of beef jerky because inserting a digital thermometer into a stiff and thin sliced piece of meat can be challenging. I wait until the 3- to 4-hour mark and do a texture test.

STORAGE: Store covered in the plastic bag on the counter for 4 to 5 days or for 2 weeks in the refrigerator.

Smoked Herbed Potatoes

**SERVES: 4 / PREP TIME: 30 MINUTES / SMOKE TIME: 2 HOURS /
RECOMMENDED WOOD: APPLE OR CHERRY**

Seasoned with dill, Italian seasoning, and Parmesan cheese, this side dish recipe makes for a delicious addition to any meal.

2 tablespoons extra-virgin olive oil

6 garlic cloves, chopped

½ teaspoon dried oregano

½ teaspoon dried basil

½ teaspoon dried dill

½ teaspoon sea salt

½ teaspoon Italian seasoning

¼ teaspoon freshly ground black pepper

1 (1½-pound) bag Gemstone or fingerling potatoes

2 tablespoons water

¼ cup Parmesan cheese, freshly grated

Chopped fresh parsley, for garnish

1. In a large bowl, combine the olive oil, garlic, oregano, basil, dill, salt, Italian seasoning, and pepper. Pour the marinade into a large plastic bag.

2. Rinse the potatoes and put them into the marinade.

3. Shake the bag to coat the potatoes. Put the plastic bag in the refrigerator to marinate for at least 2 hours and up to 4 hours.

4. Create a foil pouch by tearing off a piece of 18-by-18-inch heavy-duty foil. Lay it on a flat surface. Put the potatoes and water in the center of the foil. Then, fold the 4 sides of the foil over top of the potatoes to completely enclose them. Use a fork to poke 4 to 6 small holes in the top of the foil so air and smoke can circulate.

5. Prepare the smoker and preheat until the internal temperature reaches 225°F.

6. Put the foil pouch directly on the smoker racks and smoke for 2 hours. Once done, remove the foil pouch and let rest for 5 minutes before opening.

7. Slowly open the pouch and pour the potatoes into a bowl.

8. Top with the Parmesan cheese and chopped parsley.

Smoked Macaroni and Cheese

SERVES: 6 TO 8 / **PREP TIME:** 30 MINUTES / **SMOKE TIME:** 2 HOURS /
RECOMMENDED WOOD: HICKORY

This macaroni and cheese recipe is a classic and when smoked, it provides a wonderful flavor that tastes great with so many smoked meats.

I always put the pan of macaroni and cheese directly under the meat I'm smoking because the drippings from the smoked meat land on top of the macaroni and cheese and intensify the flavor.

1 (1-pound) box elbow macaroni noodles

1 (1-pound) block Velveeta cheese, cubed

1 cup 2% milk

8 tablespoons (1 stick) cold salted butter

Kosher salt

Freshly ground black pepper

1. Cook the elbow macaroni according to package directions. Drain in a colander and set aside.

2. Add the cooked pasta to a large pot and slowly stir in the Velveeta cheese, milk, and butter.

3. Cook on medium heat, continuously stirring until the cheese has melted. Add salt and pepper to taste.

4. Pour the macaroni and cheese into a disposable aluminum pan.

5. Prepare the smoker and preheat until the internal temperature reaches 225°F.

6. Put the uncovered aluminum pan on the smoker racks.

7. Smoke for 1½ hours, or until the top becomes golden brown. Serve immediately.

EASY INGREDIENT TIP: If you like a bit of spicy, mix some melted Pepper Jack cheese in with the Velveeta cheese.

Smoked Cherry Tomatoes with Basil and Goat Cheese

SERVES: 6 TO 8 / PREP TIME: 15 MINUTES (PLUS UP TO 2 HOURS TO MARINATE) /
SMOKE TIME: 1 HOUR / RECOMMENDED WOOD: APPLE OR ALDER

Smoked cherry tomatoes are the perfect side dish for any meal, especially seafood. It only takes 15 minutes for an easy prep with a showstopper taste, and you'll have yourself one simple and healthy side dish!

25 to 30 cherry tomatoes

2 tablespoons extra-virgin olive oil

1 tablespoon balsamic vinegar

¼ cup crumbled goat cheese, plus extra for topping

⅛ cup fresh basil, sliced, plus extra for topping

¼ teaspoon kosher salt

¼ teaspoon freshly ground black pepper

1 tablespoon water

1. Rinse the cherry tomatoes and put them in a large bowl.

2. In a gallon-size resealable plastic bag, put the tomatoes, olive oil, balsamic vinegar, goat cheese, basil, salt, and pepper.

3. Seal the bag and shake well to combine all the ingredients, then marinate in the refrigerator for at least 2 hours.

4. Create a foil pouchby tearing off a piece of 18-by-18-inch heavy-duty foil.

5. Lay the foil on a flat surface and put the tomatoes in the center. Add the water.

6. Fold the 4 sides of the foil over the tomatoes so that they are completely enclosed.

7. Use a fork to poke 4 to 6 small holes in the top of the foil so air and smoke can circulate.

8. Prepare the smoker and preheat until the internal temperature reaches 225°F.

9. Put the foil pouch directly on the smoker racks and smoke for 1 hour.

CONTINUED ▶

10. Once done, remove the tomatoes and let rest for 3 minutes.

11. Open up the pocket and pour the tomatoes into a bowl.

12. Top the smoked tomatoes with basil and goat cheese crumbles. Serve immediately.

Homestyle Barbecue Sauce

MAKES: 4 CUPS / PREP TIME: 10 MINUTES / COOK TIME: 20 MINUTES

If you've never made homemade barbecue sauce, start with this recipe because it is easy to make and has irresistible sweet and smoky flavors. The key ingredients here are the smoked paprika and strong-brewed coffee. The paprika brings out the smoky flavor while the coffee pulls out the bold flavors that help cut some of the sweetness. Using a dark-roast coffee works best in this recipe. This barbecue sauce tastes great with many different types of meat, but I enjoy this one most on chicken wings, chicken breasts, and ribs.

2 cups ketchup

½ cup apple cider vinegar

½ cup honey

¼ cup strong-brewed coffee

½ cup packed light brown sugar

½ tablespoon smoked paprika

½ tablespoon chili powder

½ tablespoon minced garlic

½ tablespoon minced onion

½ tablespoon dried parsley

1. In a large saucepan, combine the ketchup, apple cider vinegar, honey, coffee, brown sugar, paprika, chili powder, garlic, onion, and parsley. Bring to a low-rolling boil over medium-high heat.

2. Reduce the heat to medium-low when it starts to boil.

3. Once the sauce starts to get thick, after about 15 minutes, remove from the heat.

EASY COOKING TIP: If you like a thicker barbecue sauce, turn up the heat and boil for an additional 5 to 10 minutes. The key to thickening this sauce is to let it get hot while at a consistent boil.

STORAGE: Put any leftovers in an airtight container and refrigerate for up to 3 weeks. Ensure that the sauce is fully cooled before storing.

St. Louis–Style Barbecue Sauce

MAKES: 4 CUPS / PREP TIME: 10 MINUTES / COOK TIME: 35 MINUTES (PLUS 20 TO 30 MINUTES TO COOL)

When it comes to barbecue sauces, you'll quickly find that there are many different types and flavors available. When I hear "St. Louis–Style," I often think of ribs because St. Louis–style spare ribs are popular. St. Louis–style barbecue sauce is described by author Steven Raichlen as a "very sweet, slightly acidic, sticky, tomato-based barbecue sauce," which is why this style barbecue sauce is so good on ribs. And you typically won't find liquid smoke in this style of barbecue sauce like you will in other styles. True to Raichlen's description, the ingredients in my recipe meet the flavor criteria, and the sauce is great on so many different meats. But let me tell you—I do love it on ribs!

3 cups ketchup

½ cup water

½ cup apple cider vinegar

½ cup packed dark brown sugar

¼ cup yellow mustard

2 tablespoons Worcestershire sauce

1 tablespoon minced onion

2 teaspoons garlic powder

1 teaspoon kosher salt

¼ teaspoon cayenne pepper

1. In a large saucepan, combine the ketchup, water, apple cider vinegar, brown sugar, mustard, Worcestershire sauce, onion, garlic powder, salt, and cayenne pepper. Bring to a low-rolling boil over medium-high heat.

2. Reduce the heat to medium-low when it starts to boil. The sauce should be thin but not watery.

3. Stir occasionally and simmer for 30 minutes, reducing the heat if it's boiling too much.

4. Allow the barbecue sauce to cool for 20 to 30 minutes before applying it to meat.

STORAGE: Put any leftovers in an airtight container and refrigerate for up to 3 weeks. Ensure that the sauce is fully cooled before storing.

Cherry Barbecue Sauce

MAKES: 4 CUPS / **PREP TIME:** 10 MINUTES / **COOK TIME:** 30 MINUTES (PLUS 20 MINUTES TO COOL)

This barbecue sauce has a subtle cherry flavor and pairs exceptionally well with duck and beef recipes. The thing I love most about this sauce is that you can taste the layers of different flavors—hints of ginger paired with the cherry base provide an enormous amount of flavor with just enough sweetness for any meat it tops. This sauce is such a crowd favorite every time I smoke meat with it that, people ask if I have any to spare! I've learned to make an extra batch so I have it on hand to pass out when people request it. It's that good!

½ cup balsamic vinegar

¼ cup packed dark brown sugar

3 tablespoons honey

3 cups pitted frozen cherries

⅓ cup apple cider vinegar

2 cups ketchup

1 tablespoon Worcestershire sauce

2 garlic cloves, minced

2 tablespoons smoked paprika

1 teaspoon dry mustard

1 teaspoon minced onions

1½ teaspoon kosher salt

½ teaspoon ground ginger

½ teaspoon red pepper flakes

½ teaspoon freshly ground black pepper

1. In a large saucepan, combine the balsamic vinegar, brown sugar, honey, cherries, and apple cider vinegar. Bring to a low-rolling boil over medium-high heat.

2. Reduce the heat to medium-low, then remove from the heat and let cool for 20 minutes.

3. Pour the sauce from the pot into a blender or food processor and puree.

4. Add the pureed ingredients back into the pot and add the ketchup, Worcestershire sauce, garlic, paprika, dry mustard, onions, salt, ginger, red pepper flakes, and pepper.

5. Bring to a boil, stirring continually, then reduce the heat to a simmer.

6. Cover and simmer on medium-low heat for 20 minutes. Let cool.

STORAGE: Put any leftovers in an airtight container and refrigerate for up to 3 weeks. Ensure that the sauce is fully cooled before storing.

Kansas City–Style Barbecue Sauce

MAKES: 4 CUPS / PREP TIME: 10 MINUTES / COOK TIME: 35 MINUTES

If I had to choose my all-time favorite barbecue sauce, it would be this one. This style of sauce originated in Kansas City, Missouri. It is thick, sweet, and tangy and provides layers of flavor. The molasses and ketchup give this sauce a sweeter taste, and although I don't add the liquid smoke you'd typically find in this sauce, you'll be able to pick up on some subtle smoky flavors from the paprika, Worcestershire sauce, and chili powder. This barbecue sauce pairs well with chicken and pork recipes.

2 cups ketchup

⅓ cup apple cider vinegar

¼ cup packed dark brown sugar

2 tablespoons molasses

1 tablespoon Worcestershire sauce

1 tablespoon smoked paprika

2 teaspoons chili powder

1 teaspoon dry mustard

1 teaspoon garlic powder

1 teaspoon minced onions

1 teaspoon kosher salt

1 teaspoon freshly ground black pepper

1. In a large saucepan, combine the ketchup, apple cider vinegar, brown sugar, molasses, Worcestershire sauce, paprika, chili powder, dry mustard, garlic powder, onions, salt, and pepper. Bring to a low-rolling boil over medium-high heat.

2. Reduce the heat to low, cover, and simmer for 30 minutes. Let cool.

STORAGE: Put any leftovers in an airtight container and refrigerate for up to 3 weeks. Ensure that the sauce is fully cooled before storing.

Carolina Mustard Barbecue Sauce

MAKES: 4 CUPS / PREP TIME: 10 MINUTES / COOK TIME: 25 MINUTES

A little sweet, a little tangy, and a little spicy—that's the flavor combination you'll get from this barbecue sauce. Just like the other sauces in this chapter, this Carolina-originated sauce has tons of flavor, but the mustard base makes this recipe one of my favorites. I'm a huge fan of mustard, and when paired with vinegar, dark brown sugar, and ketchup, this golden sauce is delicious with chicken or pork.

¾ cup yellow mustard

⅓ cup apple cider vinegar

¼ cup honey

¼ cup packed dark brown sugar

1 tablespoon cold unsalted butter

1 tablespoon ketchup

2 teaspoons Worcestershire sauce

¼ teaspoon Tabasco sauce

1 teaspoon garlic powder

1 teaspoon onion powder

1 teaspoon dry mustard

½ teaspoon kosher salt

½ teaspoon freshly ground black pepper

¼ teaspoon cayenne pepper

1. In a large saucepan, combine the yellow mustard, apple cider vinegar, honey, brown sugar, butter, ketchup, Worcestershire sauce, Tabasco sauce, garlic powder, onion powder, dry mustard, salt, black pepper, and cayenne pepper. Bring to a low-rolling boil over medium-high heat.

2. Reduce the heat to low and simmer for 20 minutes. Let cool.

STORAGE: Put any leftovers in an airtight container and refrigerate for up to 3 weeks. Ensure that the sauce is fully cooled before storing.

Tarragon Dijon Sauce

MAKES: 1½ CUPS / PREP TIME: 10 MINUTES / COOK TIME: 20 MINUTES

Tarragon and Dijon mustard are two of my favorite ingredients, and I feature them both in this sauce. This creamy tarragon mustard sauce is versatile and excellent in so many recipes. I feature this sauce in my smoked bratwursts recipe, but I also love it paired with lamb.

1 cup heavy whipping cream

1 tablespoon Dijon mustard

2 tablespoons chopped fresh tarragon

1 teaspoon minced onion

¼ teaspoon white pepper

¼ teaspoon paprika

1. In a medium saucepan, combine the cream, mustard, tarragon, onion, pepper, and paprika. Bring to a boil over medium-high heat.

2. Reduce the heat to medium-low and cook for 15 to 20 minutes. Serve immediately.

EASY SUBSTITUTION TIP: If you can't find fresh tarragon, dried tarragon will work, too.

STORAGE: Put any leftovers in an airtight container and refrigerate for up to 3 days. Ensure that the sauce is fully cooled before storing.

Brisket Rub

MAKES: ½ CUP / PREP TIME: 10 MINUTES

How you season a brisket for smoking is so important. There are many dry rub options available, but I love the mixture of a brown sugar rub with a hint of savory and spice—and that's the flavor combination you'll get with this brisket rub. Season your brisket or brisket burnt ends with this rub for 4 hours before starting the smoking process. The flavor combination is out of this world!

¼ cup packed light brown sugar

1 tablespoon garlic powder

1 tablespoon smoked paprika

1 tablespoon seasoning salt

2 teaspoons freshly ground black pepper

1 teaspoon onion powder

1 teaspoon dried oregano

½ teaspoon ground cumin

1. In a large bowl, combine the brown sugar, garlic powder, paprika, salt, pepper, onion powder, oregano, and cumin.

2. Store the rub in an airtight container until ready to use.

STORAGE: The dry rub will last up to 6 months if stored in a cool, dry place.

House Seasoning

MAKES: 1½ **CUPS / PREP TIME:** 5 **MINUTES**

The is the most flavorful four-ingredient dry rub recipe I've ever tasted! I use this house seasoning on many different recipes, but I especially love using it on chuck roast because the dry rub helps form the best bark that's full of robust flavor. This seasoning is excellent on many smoked foods, but try using it in casseroles and on French fries!

1 cup kosher salt

¼ cup garlic powder

¼ cup freshly ground black pepper

2 tablespoons dried parsley

1. In a large bowl, combine the salt, garlic powder, pepper, and parsley.

2. Store the rub in an airtight container until ready to use.

STORAGE: The dry rub will last up to 6 months if stored in a cool, dry place.

Boston Butt Rub

MAKES: 2 CUPS / PREP TIME: 10 MINUTES

Don't just use this dry rub for smoking pork butt! This sweet and spicy rub can also be used on baby back ribs and chicken. Two types of sugar bring the sweetness while the smoked paprika, chili powder, and cayenne pepper contribute to the spiciness. Prepare a big batch in advance and store the rub in your cupboard to use on a variety of meats.

½ cup kosher salt

½ cup turbinado sugar

¼ cup packed light brown sugar

2 tablespoons smoked paprika

2 tablespoons chili powder

1½ tablespoons freshly ground black pepper

1 tablespoon garlic powder

1 tablespoon onion powder

1 tablespoon ground cumin

2 teaspoons dry mustard

½ teaspoon ground coriander

⅛ teaspoon cayenne pepper

1. In a large bowl, combine the salt, turbinado sugar, brown sugar, paprika, chili powder, black pepper, garlic powder, onion powder, cumin, dry mustard, coriander, and cayenne pepper.

2. Store the rub in an airtight container until ready to use.

STORAGE: The dry rub will last up to 6 months if stored in a cool, dry place.

Montreal Dry Rub

MAKES: ⅓ CUP / PREP TIME: 10 MINUTES

If I had to choose my favorite dry rub recipe for steak, this would be it! I crush the whole peppercorns with a meat cleaver and then add the pepper to the other ingredients. The addition of dried dill and ground coriander makes this dry rub stand out. The flavor is restaurant quality and tastes great on rib eye, tri-tip, and New York strip.

1 tablespoon black peppercorns, crushed

1 tablespoon dry mustard

1½ tablespoons kosher salt

1½ tablespoons garlic powder

2 teaspoons dried dill

2 teaspoons smoked paprika

1 teaspoon coriander

1 teaspoon red pepper flakes

1. In a large bowl, combine the peppercorns, dry mustard, salt, garlic powder, dill, paprika, coriander, and red pepper flakes.

2. Store the rub in an airtight container until ready to use.

EASY PREP TIP: To crush whole peppercorns, put them in a resealable plastic bag, removing any air before closing. Take a meat tenderizer or rolling pin and press down to crush to desired consistency.

STORAGE: The dry rub will last up to 6 months if stored in a cool, dry place.

Seafood Garlic Butter Sauce

MAKES: ½ CUP / PREP TIME: 10 MINUTES

Seafood is delicate and doesn't need a lot of extra flavor, but the addition of butter, garlic, and lemon juice topped with freshly ground pepper adds a subtle finish to lobster, crab legs, scallops, and other types of fish. This is my go-to seafood sauce when basting seafood during the smoking process as well as my favorite dipping sauce after the smoking is done. Just make sure you don't use the same batch of sauce you basted with for dipping!

8 tablespoons (1 stick) unsalted butter, at room temperature

3 garlic cloves, minced

⅛ teaspoon freshly ground black pepper

Juice of ½ lemon

1. In a large bowl, combine the butter, garlic, pepper, and lemon juice.

2. Use this mixture as a baste while smoking meat or as a dipping sauce.

STORAGE: Put any leftovers in an airtight container and refrigerate for up to 5 days.

Tzatziki Sauce

MAKES: 3 CUPS / PREP TIME: 10 MINUTES

This yogurt-based cucumber sauce is chilled and refreshingly delicious. While it tastes wonderful with smoked meats like lamb, it also tastes great with vegetables and pita bread. The dill and lemon juice provide a burst of fresh flavor that complements so many foods!

2 cups plain Greek yogurt

¾ cup English cucumber, peeled and chopped

1 tablespoon extra-virgin olive oil

1 tablespoon freshly squeezed lemon juice

1 teaspoon white vinegar

5 garlic cloves

2 tablespoons chopped fresh dill

1½ teaspoons kosher salt

¼ teaspoon white pepper

1. Blend the yogurt, cucumber, olive oil, lemon juice, vinegar, garlic, dill, salt, and pepper in a food processor or blender until the ingredients are pureed and completely smooth.

2. Pour the sauce into a container with a lid and refrigerate for 2 hours.

3. Once chilled, serve.

STORAGE: Put any leftovers in an airtight container and refrigerate for up to 5 days.

Garlic Aioli

MAKES: ½ **CUP / PREP TIME:** 10 **MINUTES**

Simply put, this easy garlic mayonnaise recipe is delicious on so many different types of foods! This aioli is made with only a few ingredients you probably already have. Just mix those ingredients together and you've got yourself one delicious batch of homemade garlic mayonnaise.

6 tablespoons mayonnaise

2 tablespoons extra-virgin olive oil

1 teaspoon freshly squeezed lemon juice

2 garlic cloves, minced

Freshly ground black pepper

1. In a small mixing bowl, whisk together the mayonnaise, olive oil, lemon juice, and garlic.

2. Season with pepper and serve.

STORAGE: Put any leftovers in an airtight container and refrigerate for up to 1 week.

MEASUREMENT CONVERSIONS

VOLUME EQUIVALENTS (LIQUID)

US STANDARD	US STANDARD (OUNCES)	METRIC (APPROXIMATE)
2 tablespoons	1 fl. oz.	30 mL
¼ cup	2 fl. oz.	60 mL
½ cup	4 fl. oz.	120 mL
1 cup	8 fl. oz.	240 mL
1½ cups	12 fl. oz.	355 mL
2 cups or 1 pint	16 fl. oz.	475 mL
4 cups or 1 quart	32 fl. oz.	1 L
1 gallon	128 fl. oz.	4 L

OVEN TEMPERATURES

FAHRENHEIT	CELSIUS (APPROXIMATE)
250°F	120°C
300°F	150°C
325°F	165°C
350°F	180°C
375°F	190°C
400°F	200°C
425°F	220°C
450°F	230°C

VOLUME EQUIVALENTS (DRY)

US STANDARD	METRIC (APPROXIMATE)
⅛ teaspoon	0.5 mL
¼ teaspoon	1 mL
½ teaspoon	2 mL
¾ teaspoon	4 mL
1 teaspoon	5 mL
1 tablespoon	15 mL
¼ cup	59 mL
⅓ cup	79 mL
½ cup	118 mL
⅔ cup	156 mL
¾ cup	177 mL
1 cup	235 mL
2 cups or 1 pint	475 mL
3 cups	700 mL
4 cups or 1 quart	1 L

WEIGHT EQUIVALENTS

US STANDARD	METRIC (APPROXIMATE)
½ ounce	15 g
1 ounce	30 g
2 ounces	60 g
4 ounces	115 g
8 ounces	225 g
12 ounces	340 g
16 ounces or 1 pound	455 g

REFERENCES

A. A. Newton. "You Don't Need to Truss a Turkey." November 14, 2018. skillet.lifehacker.com/you-dont-need-to-truss-a-turkey-1830411577.

Bruce Aidells. *The Great Meat Cookbook: Including Expert Advice on Sustainable Meat.* New York, New York: Mifflin Harcourt Publishing Company, 2012.

David Haug. "What Wood Not to Use For Smoking." Wisconsin Firewood. March 13, 2017. WisconsinFirewood.com/blog/what-wood-not-to-use-for-smoking.

Donna Read. "Storage of Unused Wood." Smokinlicious. May 2007. Smokinlicious.com/blog/storage-of-unused-wood.

"Do You Need to Soak Wood Chips? And Other Tips to Get the Ideal Smoke." Napoleon. Accessed April 2020. Napoleon.com/en/us/grills/do-you-need-soak-wood-chips-and-other-tips-get-ideal-smoke.

Emma Christensen. "Use a Quick Brine to Make Any Cut More Tender." Kitchn. April 14, 2008. thekitchn.com/use-a-quick-brine-to-make-any-cut-more-tender-47879.

"Grill Guide: The Offset Smoker." Kingsford. Accessed April 2020. Kingsford.com/gear/offset-smoker.

"How to Build a Slow-Burning Fire for Smoking Barbecue Meat." YouTube. September 22, 2011. YouTube.com/watch?v=0tPzZ6Y9YbU.

"How to Turn Your Charcoal Grill into a Smoker." YouTube. 1:37. Chow Tip. July 22, 2010. YouTube.com/watch?v=C6IL9tUDQlc.

Jeff Phillips, "How to Make a Foil Woodchip Pack." Accessed May 2020. Smoking-Meat.com/how-to-make-a-foil-woodchip-pack.

Joe Clements. "How to Get a Good Bark When Smoking Meat." Smoked Barbecue Source. November 20, 2017. SmokedBBQSource.com/how-to-get-a-good-bark.

Kelli Foster. "Inside the Spice Cabinet: Garlic Powder." Kitchn. October 1, 2016. thekitchn.com/inside-the-spice-cabinet-garlic-powder-103636.

Mark Jenner, "How to Turn a Gas Grill into a Smoker—It's Easy, and Super Effective!" Food Fire Friends. April 25, 2020. FoodFireFriends.com/how-turn-gas-grill-into-smoker.

Mark Jenner. "Smoker Water Pans—Why, When and How to Use One." Food Fire Friends. Last modified June 23, 2020. FoodFireFriends.com/water-pan-use.

Martin Earl. "Thermal Tips: How to Smoke a Whole Duck." *ThermoWorks* (blog). Accessed May 2020. blog.thermoworks.com/poultry/thermal-tips-smoke-duck.

Martin Earl. "Thermal Tips: Simple Roasted Chicken—Cooking Chicken to the Correct Temperature." *ThermoWorks* (blog). Accessed April 2020. blog.thermoworks.com/chicken/thermal-tips-simple-roasted-chicken.

Meathead Goldwyn. "The Science of Rubs." Amazing Ribs. Last modified March 26, 2020. AmazingRibs.com/tested-recipes/spice-rubs-and-pastes/science-rubs.

"Meat Smoking Guide | Cave Tools." Accessed April 2020. CaveTools.com/products/meat-smoking-guide.

"Pellet Grills 101." Pitboss Grills. Accessed April 2020. Kingsford.com/gear/offset-smoker.

Rachel Blackburn. "Sidekick vs. Sear Box." Camp Chef. October 23, 2019. CampChef.com/blog/sidekick-vs-sear-box.

"Safe Minimum Cooking Temperatures Charts." Last modified April 12, 2019. FoodSafety.gov/food-safety-charts/safe-minimum-cooking-temperature.

Steak University. "Prime Rib vs. Ribeye: Choices, Choices." Accessed May 5, 2020. MyChicagoSteak.com/steak-university/prime-rib-vs-ribeye.

Steven Raichlen. "How to Control the Heat on a Charcoal Grill." Barbecue Bible. April 29, 2016. BarbecueBible.com/2016/04/29/crash-course-4-ways -to-control-the-heat-on-a-charcoal-grill.

"Traeger Wood Pellet Grills Owner's Manual BBQ075.02." Traeger Grills. Accessed April 2020. TraegerGrills.com/on/demandware.static/-/Library -Sites-TraegerSharedLibrary/default/dwed6e5849/manuals/DOC095 _BBQ075.02_Texas_Pro_Blue.pdf.

United States Department of Agriculture. "Is Pink Turkey Meat Safe?" Last modified August 2, 2013. fsis.usda.gov/wps/portal/fsis/topics/food-safety -education/get-answers/food-safety-fact-sheets/poultry-preparation/is-pink -turkey-meat-safe_.

Wikipedia. "St. Louis–Style Barbecue." Accessed May 2020. en.wikipedia.org /wiki/St._Louis-style_barbecue.

Yasmin Fahr. "Cooking Temperatures, Simplified." The Daily Meal. July 11, 2011. TheDailyMeal.com/cooking-temperatures-simplified.

"Your Complete Guide to Buying an Offset Smoker." Burning Brisket BBQ Everything. Accessed April 2020. BurningBrisket.com/guide-to-buying-an -offset-smoker.

INDEX

A

Applewood Smoked
        Chicken, 100–101

B

Smoked Baby Back
        Ribs, 59–60
Bacon
        Bacon-Wrapped Smoked
                Scallops, 124–125
        Candied Barbecue
                Smoked Bacon, 40–41
        Smoked Baked Beans
                with Bacon, 138
Beans, Smoked Baked,
        with Bacon, 138
Beef, 65
        Cracked Pepper Beef
                Jerky, 139–140
        Filet Mignon & Veggie
                Kebabs, 75–76
        Five-Spice Beef Short
                Ribs, 80–81
        Montreal Rib Eye, 69
        Peppercorn-Crusted Beef
                Sirloin Tip Roast, 68
        Santa Maria–Style
                Smoked Tri-Tip
                Steak, 77
        Smoked Brisket, 84–85
        Smoked Brisket Burnt
                Ends with Cherry
                Barbecue
                Sauce, 86–87
        Smoked Chuck
                Roast, 88
        Smoked Marinated Flank
                Steak, 66
        Smoked Prime Rib, 73

smoking chart, 23–26
Sweet and Spicy
        Cheese-Stuffed
        Smoked
        Meatloaf, 82–83
Blackened Smoked
        Catfish, 119
Smoked Boston Butt, 61–62
Boston Butt Rub, 155
Brining, 20
Brisket Rub, 153
        Smoked Brisket, 84–85
        Smoked Brisket Burnt
                Ends with Cherry
                Barbecue
                Sauce, 86–87

C

Cajun Smoked Whole
        Chicken, 107–108
Candied Barbecue Smoked
        Bacon, 40–41
Carolina Mustard Barbecue
        Sauce, 151
        Candied Barbecue
                Smoked Bacon, 40–41
        Carolina Mustard Smoked
                Chicken Thighs, 97
Carolina Mustard Smoked
        Chicken Thighs, 97
Catfish, Blackened
        Smoked, 119
Charcoal smokers,
        5, 7, 11–12
Cheese
        Parmesan Couscous–
                Stuffed Smoked
                Quail, 114–115
        Parmesan-Crusted

Smoked Tilapia, 133
Smoked Cherry Tomatoes
        with Basil and Goat
        Cheese, 143–144
Smoked Herbed
        Potatoes, 141
Smoked Macaroni and
        Cheese, 142
Smoked Mahi-Mahi Soft
        Tacos with Corn
        Salsa, 131–132
Smoked Mediterranean
        Lamb Burgers, 67
Sweet and Spicy
        Cheese-Stuffed
        Smoked
        Meatloaf, 82–83
Cherry Barbecue Sauce, 149
        Cherry Barbecue Smoked
                Duck, 112–113
        Five-Spice Beef Short
                Ribs, 80–81
        Smoked Brisket Burnt
                Ends with Cherry
                Barbecue
                Sauce, 86–87
Cherry Barbecue Smoked
        Duck, 112–113
Chicken, 92
        Applewood Smoked
                Chicken, 100–101
        Cajun Smoked Whole
                Chicken, 107–108
        Carolina Mustard Smoked
                Chicken Thighs, 97
        Herbed Smoked Chicken
                Quarters, 102
        Hickory Smoked
                Barbecue Chicken
                Breasts, 98–99

Smoked Buffalo Chicken
Wings, 93
Smoked Chicken
Drumsticks, 96
smoking chart, 27–28
Sweet and Tangy
Barbecue Smoked
Chicken Wings,
94–95
Coconut Shrimp,
Smoked, 128
Cornish hens
Honey-Orange Smoked
Cornish Hen, 103
smoking chart, 28
Corn Salsa, Smoked
Mahi-Mahi Soft Tacos
with, 131–132
Crab Legs, Smoked, 134
Cracked Pepper Beef
Jerky, 139–140
Cucumbers
Tzatziki Sauce, 158
Curing, 20

D

Doneness, 32, 92
Duck
Cherry Barbecue Smoked
Duck, 112–113
smoking chart, 28

E

Electric smokers, 5, 7, 15
Equipment, 3, 15–17

F

Filet Mignon & Veggie
Kebabs, 75–76
Fires, building and
feeding, 11–15
Fish, 117
Blackened Smoked
Catfish, 119

Orange-Ginger Smoked
Halibut, 126 127
Orange Honey-Glazed
Smoked
Salmon, 121–122
Parmesan-Crusted
Smoked Tilapia, 133
Smoked Ahi Tuna, 123
Smoked Mahi-Mahi Soft
Tacos with Corn
Salsa, 131–132
smoking chart, 28–29
Five-Spice Beef Short
Ribs, 80–81
Flavoring
meats, 19–21
with woods, 9–10, 31
Fuel sources, 7–11

G

Garlic Aioli, 159
Smoked Chorizo Links
with Garlic Aioli, 38
Garlic Butter Smoked
Shrimp, 118
Garlic-Crusted Smoked
Rack of Lamb, 72
Garlic-Herb Smoked
Pork Loin, 48–49
Garlic-Rosemary Smoked
Lamb Chops, 71
Gas smokers, 7–8, 13, 30, 33
Grills, 6

H

Halibut, Orange-Ginger
Smoked, 126–127
Ham
Pineapple-Glazed
Smoked Ham, 45–46
Smoked Ham
Hocks, 52–53
Smoked Pit Ham,
42–43

Herbed Smoked Chicken
Quarters, 102
Herb Smoked Pork
Chops, 47
Hickory Smoked Barbecue
Chicken Breasts, 98–99
Homestyle Barbecue
Sauce, 147
Smoked Baby Back
Ribs, 59–60
Honey-Orange Smoked
Cornish Hen, 103
House Seasoning, 154
Peppercorn-Crusted Beef
Sirloin Tip Roast, 68
Smoked Chuck Roast, 88

I

Ingredient staples, 17–19
Injections, 20

K

Kansas City–Style
Barbecue Sauce, 150
Kansas City–Style
Barbecue Smoked
Pork Belly Burnt
Ends, 54–55
Sweet and Spicy
Cheese-Stuffed
Smoked
Meatloaf, 82–83
Sweet and Tangy
Barbecue Smoked
Chicken Wings,
94–95
Kansas City–Style Barbecue
Smoked Pork Belly
Burnt Ends, 54–55

L

Lamb, 65
Garlic-Crusted Smoked
Rack of Lamb, 72
Garlic-Rosemary Smoked
Lamb Chops, 71

Lamb (*continued*)
Smoked Lamb Shoulder
with Au Jus, 78–79
Smoked Mediterranean
Lamb Burgers, 67
smoking chart, 26–27
Lobster Tail, Smoked, 129

M

Macaroni and Cheese,
Smoked, 142
Mahi-Mahi, Smoked, Soft
Tacos with Corn
Salsa, 131–132
Marinades, 20, 33. *See
also* Sauces
Meats. *See also* Smoking
meat; *specific*
doneness, 32
fat trimming, 33
flipping, 33
purchasing, 32, 34
smoking charts, 21–29
Montreal Dry Rub, 156
Filet Mignon & Veggie
Kebabs, 75–76
Montreal Rib Eye, 69
Montreal Rib Eye, 69
Mushrooms
Filet Mignon & Veggie
Kebabs, 75–76

O

Onions
Filet Mignon & Veggie
Kebabs, 75–76
Orange-Ginger Smoked
Halibut, 126–127
Orange Honey-Glazed
Smoked Salmon,
121–122

P

Pantry staples, 17–19

Parmesan Couscous–
Stuffed Smoked
Quail, 114–115
Parmesan-Crusted
Smoked Tilapia, 133
Pellet smokers, 4, 5, 8, 15
Peppercorn-Crusted Beef
Sirloin Tip Roast, 68
Peppers
Filet Mignon & Veggie
Kebabs, 75–76
Smoked Mahi-Mahi Soft
Tacos with Corn
Salsa, 131–132
Pineapples and
pineapple juice
Filet Mignon & Veggie
Kebabs, 75–76
Pineapple-Glazed
Smoked Ham, 45–46
Smoked Pit Ham, 42–43
Pork, 31, 33, 37
Smoked Baby Back
Ribs, 59–60
Smoked Boston
Butt, 61–62
Candied Barbecue
Smoked Bacon, 40–41
Garlic-Herb Smoked Pork
Loin, 48–49
Herb Smoked Pork
Chops, 47
Kansas City–Style
Barbecue Smoked
Pork Belly Burnt
Ends, 54–55
Pineapple-Glazed
Smoked Ham, 45–46
Smoked Boneless Pork
Tenderloin, 50–51
Smoked Bratwursts with
Sauerkraut and
Tarragon Dijon
Sauce, 39
Smoked Chorizo Links
with Garlic Aioli, 38

Smoked Ham
Hocks, 52–53
Smoked Pit Ham, 42–43
smoking chart, 22
St. Louis–Style Smoked
Spare Ribs, 57–58
Sweet and Spicy
Cheese-Stuffed
Smoked
Meatloaf, 82–83
Potatoes, Smoked
Herbed, 141
Poultry, 27–28, 91–92.
See also specific
Propane gas smokers, 5

Q

Quail
Parmesan Couscous–
Stuffed Smoked
Quail, 114–115
smoking chart, 28

R

Recipes, about, 34
Roasted Herb Smoked
Whole Turkey,
110–111
Rubs, 3, 20
Boston Butt Rub, 155
Brisket Rub, 153
House Seasoning, 154
Montreal Dry Rub, 156

S

Safety, 10–11, 37, 92
Salmon, Orange Honey-
Glazed Smoked,
121–122
Santa Maria–Style Smoked
Tri-Tip Steak, 77
Sauces, 3
Carolina Mustard
Barbecue Sauce, 151

Cherry Barbecue
Sauce, 149

Garlic Aioli, 159

Homestyle Barbecue
Sauce, 147

Kansas City–Style
Barbecue Sauce, 150

Seafood Garlic Butter
Sauce, 157

St. Louis–Style Barbecue
Sauce, 148

Tarragon Dijon
Sauce, 152

Tzatziki Sauce, 158

Sauerkraut and Tarragon
Dijon Sauce, Smoked
Bratwursts with, 39

Sausage
Smoked Bratwursts with
Sauerkraut and
Tarragon Dijon Sauce, 39

Smoked Chorizo Links
with Garlic Aioli, 38

Scallops, Bacon-Wrapped
Smoked, 124–125

Seafood, 117. See also Fish
Bacon-Wrapped Smoked
Scallops, 124–125

Garlic Butter Smoked
Shrimp, 118

Smoked Coconut
Shrimp, 128

Smoked Crab Legs, 134

Smoked Lobster Tail, 129

smoking chart, 28–29

Seafood Garlic Butter
Sauce, 157

Garlic Butter Smoked
Shrimp, 118

Smoked Crab Legs, 134

Smoked Lobster Tail, 129

Seasoning smokers, 30–31

Shrimp

Garlic Butter Smoked
Shrimp, 118

Smoked Coconut
Shrimp, 128

Sides
Smoked Baked Beans
with Bacon, 138

Smoked Cherry Tomatoes
with Basil and Goat
Cheese, 143–144

Smoked Herbed
Potatoes, 141

Smoked Macaroni and
Cheese, 142

Smoke, 3, 14, 31. See
also Fires, building
and feeding

Smoked Ahi Tuna, 123

Smoked Baked Beans
with Bacon, 138

Smoked Boneless Pork
Tenderloin, 50–51

Smoked Bratwursts
with Sauerkraut
and Tarragon
Dijon Sauce, 39

Smoked Brisket, 84–85

Smoked Brisket Burnt Ends
with Cherry Barbecue
Sauce, 86–87

Smoked Buffalo Chicken
Wings, 93

Smoked Cherry Tomatoes
with Basil and Goat
Cheese, 143–144

Smoked Chicken
Drumsticks, 96

Smoked Chorizo Links
with Garlic Aioli, 38

Smoked Chuck Roast, 88

Smoked Coconut
Shrimp, 128

Smoked Crab Legs, 134

Smoked Ham Hocks, 52–53

Smoked Herbed
Potatoes, 141

Smoked Lamb Shoulder
with Au Jus, 78–79

Smoked Lobster Tail, 129

Smoked Macaroni and
Cheese, 142

Smoked Mahi-Mahi Soft
Tacos with Corn
Salsa, 131–132

Smoked Marinated
Flank Steak, 66

Smoked Mediterranean
Lamb Burgers, 67

Smoked Pit Ham, 42–43

Smoked Prime Rib, 73

Smoked Turkey Breast
with Butter Herb
Glaze, 105–106

Smokers, types of, 3–5

Smoking meat
about, 1–2

building and feeding
fire, 11–15

charts, 21–29

equipment, 15–17

frequently asked
questions, 30–34

fuel sources, 7–11

keys to success, 2–3

with a standard grill, 6

types of smokers, 3–5

woods, 7–11

Spatchcocking, 92

Stalls, 31

St. Louis–Style Barbecue
Sauce, 148

Hickory Smoked
Barbecue Chicken
Breasts, 98–99

Smoked Boneless Pork
Tenderloin, 50–51

St. Louis–Style Smoked
Spare Ribs, 57–58

St. Louis–Style Smoked
Spare Ribs, 57–58
Sweet and Spicy Cheese-
Stuffed Smoked
Meatloaf, 82–83
Sweet and Tangy Barbecue
Smoked Chicken
Wings, 94–95

T

Tarragon Dijon Sauce, 152
Smoked Bratwursts with
Sauerkraut and
Tarragon Dijon
Sauce, 39
Temperature, 2–3, 31, 33, 92

"Thin blue smoke," 14
Tilapia, Parmesan-Crusted
Smoked, 133
Time, 2
Tomatoes
Filet Mignon & Veggie
Kebabs, 75–76
Smoked Cherry Tomatoes
with Basil and Goat
Cheese, 143–144
Smoked Mahi-Mahi Soft
Tacos with Corn
Salsa, 131–132
Tools, 15–17
Trussing, 92
Tuna, Smoked Ahi, 123

Turkey
Roasted Herb Smoked
Whole Turkey, 110–111
Smoked Turkey Breast
with Butter Herb
Glaze, 105–106
smoking chart, 27–28
Tzatziki Sauce, 158

W

Woods, 3, 7–11, 30

Y

Yogurt
Tzatziki Sauce, 158

ACKNOWLEDGMENTS

First and foremost, to God be the glory. I'm blessed that I get to share my talents worldwide with others so they can create delicious food for their families and loved ones.

I want to thank my amazingly supportive husband, Greg, for all he's done to help me get where I am today. I could not have done any of this without your love and support. As I was developing countless recipes and typing away behind a computer for endless hours week after week, you're there cleaning, washing all the dishes, and taking care of the kids while still encouraging me every step of the way. You're my motivator. I love you and I hope you know how much your words, actions, and behaviors inspire me to keep going.

To my two absolutely beautiful children, my pride and joy, Kyliegh and Davis. Words can't express what you mean to me and how proud I am to be your mom. No matter what I do in life, you both will always be my greatest accomplishments. Thank you for allowing me to live my dreams while building memories for us and building our future.

A special thanks to my nephew, Tyree, who has always encouraged me in everything I do. Your words and honesty resonate with me more than you'll ever know. I'm so appreciative to have you in my life. Credit goes to you for helping me develop some amazing recipes based on your feedback. You have an amazing palate. I love you, nephew!

To Anthony, who has become part of our family and our best friend. You're always there for me and pushing me to evolve and grow. I'm forever thankful for you—we love you.

To my mom, who was there with me during each recipe creation, tasting and providing feedback, along with cleaning up after me and washing multiple loads of dishes. For my entire life, you have always been there supporting me along the way in everything I do. If it weren't for the principles and values you instilled in me from an early age, I would not be where I am today. I'm sincerely grateful for that. I love you, Mom.

To my daddy, my smoking buddy, who has given me so many memories. I love our Peach family heritage. Thank you for teaching me all you know about the art of smoking food. If it weren't for you, this book would not be a reality. So, this one is for you. I love you, Daddy.

To Lyndsay, for years of friendship, support, and a ton of encouragement.

To my weekend taste-testers: Anthony, Lisa, Greg, Tyree, Kathy, Bobby, Kyliegh, and Davis. We'll always have our Sunday night dinners! And for Jami, Dallas, Gage, Dasia, Jackson, Amy, Neal, Kate, Patience, and Sandra. Your feedback went into a lot of these recipes!

A special thanks to Blake and Franz, who are a part of my Unicon family, for allowing me to pursue my dreams on top of all my other responsibilities. I am forever thankful to you both. Your support has changed my family's future, and I could not be more grateful.

A huge thank-you to my publishing company and editing team! You guys are amazing!

And to all my loyal followers on my food blog, *Recipes Worth Repeating*, I am forever grateful for each of you. Thank you for supporting me in my recipe creations.

ABOUT THE AUTHOR

 **AMANDA MASON** is the founder and creator behind *Recipes Worth Repeating*, a food blog that was launched in 2012 and features simple, delicious, family-focused recipes. While she began cooking at a young age, Amanda started working at a local restaurant, Franklin Chop House, at the age of 15, leading her to become even more passionate about cooking and food preparation. Her recipes and writings have been featured in numerous places, both in print and online, including *Taste of Home*, MSN, SheKnows.com, BravoTV.com, and many more. Born and raised outside of Nashville, Tennessee, she now lives with her husband and two children in Phoenix, Arizona. Visit her website at RecipesWorthRepeating.com.